Evaluation of a Trauma-Informed Program for Juvenile Justice-Involved Youth

The Pilot Program at Lookout Mountain Youth Services Center

STEPHANIE BROOKS HOLLIDAY, JIRKA TAYLOR, PRISCILLIA HUNT, IFEANYI EDOCHIE, SARAH B. HUNTER

Prepared for the Colorado Department of Human Services

For more information on this publication, visit www.rand.org/t/RR4219

Library of Congress Cataloging-in-Publication Data is available for this publication.
ISBN: 978-1-9774-0417-6

Published by the RAND Corporation, Santa Monica, Calif.
© Copyright 2020 RAND Corporation
RAND® is a registered trademark.

Support RAND
Make a tax-deductible charitable contribution at
www.rand.org/giving/contribute

www.rand.org

Preface

There is increasing recognition of the prevalence of trauma exposure among youth involved in the juvenile justice system. To better address the needs of these youth, and in an effort to mitigate negative downstream consequences of their behavior (e.g., use of seclusion and restraint for disciplinary purposes, youth recidivism), there have been efforts to develop trauma-informed programming for juvenile justice-involved youth.

The Colorado Division of Youth Services (DYS) contracted with RAND Corporation to evaluate a trauma-informed pilot program being implemented in one of their residential youth facilities. This report presents the results of a process and outcome evaluation focused on the first year of implementation of the pilot program. Interested stakeholders for this report include the DYS and the General Assembly of the State of Colorado, staff of the facility where the program is being implemented, parents of youth committed to the facility, and other jurisdictions that may be interested in developing or adopting similar programs.

The research reported here was conducted in the RAND Justice Policy Program, which is part of RAND Social and Economic Well-Being, a division of the RAND Corporation that seeks to actively improve the health and social and economic well-being of populations and communities throughout the world. The program focuses on such topics as access to justice, policing, corrections, drug policy, and court system reform, as well as other policy concerns pertaining to public safety and criminal and civil justice.

Questions or comments about this report should be sent to the project leader, Stephanie Brooks Holliday (holliday@rand.org). For more information about RAND Justice Policy, see https://www.rand.org/well-being/justice-policy.html or contact justicepolicy@rand.org.

Summary

In June 2017, Colorado House Bill (HB) 17-1329 was introduced and signed into law. This legislation sought to further promote a more rehabilitative culture within the Colorado Division of Youth Services (DYS). One key component of this statute was the creation of a pilot program within DYS using a therapeutic, group-treatment approach that integrates trauma-responsive principles. The goal of this pilot program was to reduce the use of punitive practices, including seclusion and mechanical restraints; promote the physical and psychological safety of youth and staff; and, ultimately, to reduce recidivism.

The pilot program was implemented at Lookout Mountain Youth Services Center (LMYSC), one of two DYS secure facilities that exclusively serve committed youth. Key elements of the pilot program were a humane, homelike environment; use of small group processes to provide treatment; avoiding physical management and restraint; phasing out the use of certain restraint methods and seclusion completely within the first year of implementation; and ensuring staff were trained to provide trauma-responsive care. To support the first year of implementation, the Missouri Youth Service Institute (MYSI) was selected to serve as facilitators, coaches, and trainers to the pilot program.

In addition to establishing the pilot program, HB 17-1329 required that the program be evaluated to assess its effectiveness during its first year of implementation. The goals of the evaluation included the following: (1) document the initial year of implementation of the pilot program, including the nature of the program, barriers and facilitators to implementation, and resources needed to sustain or expand the pilot program; (2) determine whether the pilot program was effective in reducing the number of negative incidents (e.g., fights, assaults, injuries, use of seclusion and restraints) and improving educational outcomes compared with a similar population of youth within DYS; (3) estimate the costs associated with implementation of the pilot program; and (4) develop recommendations to DYS regarding the pilot program, including any conclusions regarding scalability of the program.

Methods

To achieve these evaluation goals, the RAND Corporation conducted a process and outcome evaluation of the pilot program. To better understand the nature of the pilot program, we completed a series of related procedures. We conducted key informant discussions, reviewed relevant documents, and conducted a site visit to observe the facility. To understand barriers and facilitators to implementation, we conducted semistructured interviews with staff of the pilot program during the implementation year. To examine outcomes associated with the program, we were provided with administrative data regarding youth and staff. This included a focus on assessing reductions in negative youth outcomes (e.g., physical responses, use of seclusion, fights and assaults); improvements in youth education; and reductions in negative staff outcomes (e.g., grievances filed, turnover). Finally, we collected cost data in the following categories: (1) personnel costs, (2) services, (3) facility costs, (4) equipment and supplies, and (5) other costs.

Description of the Pilot Program and Implementation

The pilot program built upon existing programming at the facility. Pilot program staff received training and consulting from the MYSI consultants leading up to and during the evaluation year. This included training with an emphasis on building a positive, strong group culture on the pilot unit, and leveraging these relationships to address problem behaviors. Youth in the pilot unit attended school like other youth at the facility, but lived in a renovated building with more homelike amenities. To promote community and small group bonds, staff members implemented a number of group activities, including "circle-ups," which are spontaneous groups convened to address a specific incident or conflict that has occurred.

Qualitative interviews with staff members provided critical information about the process of implementing the pilot program. These included benefits and drawbacks of the program; barriers to implementation; facilitators of implementation; resources needed; and opportunities for improvement. A summary of the common themes in these categories is given in Table S.1.

Program Outcomes

Youth Program Outcomes

In total, data were collected on 48 pilot youth and 68 comparison youth. During the evaluation period, physical responses with mechanical restraints and Level Two physical responses were the most common outcomes. There were few significant differences between pilot youth and comparison youth with respect to most outcomes. However, youth on the pilot unit were significantly less likely to have experienced a physical response with mechanical restraints or a Level Two physical response. However, they were significantly more likely to have had criminal charges filed. Regarding educational outcomes, there were no significant differences between pilot and comparison youth in the number of credits earned or proportion of youth who earned a diploma or GED during the evaluation period.

Staff Program Outcomes

Data indicated that staff absences were common. During the pilot period, staff members on both units missed approximately three days of work per month, and about 30 percent of staff on each unit left the facility. There were no significant differences between pilot and comparison staff with respect to staff injuries, and there were no grievances/complaints or criminal charges filed against staff in either group during the evaluation period.

Cost Analysis

Based on the data provided by DYS, this study finds the setup costs of the pilot pod were an estimated $337,236. Once launched, the total cost of running the pilot pod was an estimated

Table S.1
Summary of Qualitative Findings

Category	Common Themes
Benefits of the Pilot Program	• Positive relationships between youth and staff • Ability to use relationship to manage behavioral concerns • Amenities for youth that promote normalcy
Drawbacks to the Pilot Program	• Limited behavioral management tools for more extreme situations (e.g., fights, assaults) • Safety concerns • Animosity from staff and youth from other units
Barriers to Implementation	• Short-staffed at facility and high levels of turnover • Different training for newer pilot program staff and insufficient levels of training • Facility-level issues (e.g., riot) • Difficulty reconciling state and facility policies with need to manage problematic behavior
Facilitators of Implementation	• Initial pilot training and MYSI consultants • Leadership support and relationships among staff members
Resources Needed	• Additional training, including training more tailored to different staff roles • Additional staff members with relevant experience or education
Opportunities for Improvement	• Keep youth from pilot together as much as possible • Additional programs (e.g., recreational options) • Incorporation of other evidence-based practices

$3,003,352 between July 2018 and June 2019, or about $250,279 per month. Of this total running cost, the pilot's share of facility-wide costs accounted for 85 percent ($2,567,028), with the remainder ($436,323) being costs unique to the pilot.

Conclusions

The core elements of the pilot program are consistent with trauma-informed models. Similar models, such as the Missouri Model, have been demonstrated to be effective in reducing negative youth and staff outcomes. However, the present study found few significant effects of the pilot program on outcomes of interest during the evaluation period. That said, there were a number of implementation challenges that may have contributed to the lack of significant differences. These include potential contamination effects, as staff and youth from across units interacted during the study period, and elements of trauma-informed care were being implemented across DYS facilities. Therefore, while the program holds promise, we offer the following recommendations to Colorado DYS for the ongoing implementation of the program:

1. **Develop a clear description of the Colorado Model approach to trauma-informed care and the pilot program model.** Having a well-defined program model will be key to implementing the program with fidelity into the future. Such a program model could be the basis for future fidelity monitoring effort.

2. **Ensure all pilot program staff members are trained in the program model.** This is important for establishing a shared understanding of the program across staff. Colorado DYS may also consider providing trainings tailored to individual staff roles.

3. **Address challenges in staff recruitment and retention.** Staffing issues appear to be a significant barrier to pilot program implementation. The facility could consider efforts such as increasing the applicant pool; identifying ways to retain staff (e.g., returning to previous scheduling models); and ensuring staff are well-trained and feel safe.

4. **Explore staff concerns regarding safety and the effectiveness of the program in more depth.** Staff reported that in recent months they have felt unsafe at the facility, and some staff noted that this was a marked change from the previous environment. In part, this was due to a perception that trauma-informed behavior management techniques are not effective. It will be important to explore whether this reflects additional training needs, or perhaps a need for clearer protocols for staff to follow when facing challenging situations.

5. **Consider opportunities to further develop the unique features of the pilot program.** This includes recreational options suggested by staff and an aftercare program that the facility did not fully implement in the first year. That said, the initial focus should be on implementing the pilot program with fidelity before adding new elements.

6. **Continue monitoring the implementation and outcomes of the pilot program.** As part of these efforts, Colorado DYS may consider monitoring additional relevant outcomes (e.g., youth prosocial behavior) and increasing the facility's capacity for evaluation.

Table of Contents

Preface iii

Summary v

Figures and Tables xi

Abbreviations xiii

CHAPTER ONE

Introduction 1

Colorado DYS Pilot Program 3

Present Evaluation 4

CHAPTER TWO

Method 5

Procedures 5

Data Analysis 9

CHAPTER THREE

Evaluation Results 11

Description of the Pilot Program 11

Qualitative Findings Regarding Program Implementation 18

Youth Program Outcomes 22

Staff Outcomes 26

Cost Analysis 27

CHAPTER FOUR

Conclusion 31

Summary of Findings 31

Considerations Related to Fit with Colorado DYS 33

Limitations 34

Recommendations 35

APPENDIXES

A. Supplemental Youth and Staff Results 41

B. Semistructured Interview Protocol 47

C. Additional Cost Analysis Tables 49

References 53

Figures and Tables

Figures

1.1. The Colorado Model 3
3.1. Timeline of Pilot Program Implementation 11
3.2. Pilot Program Logic Model 17

Tables

S.1. Summary of Qualitative Findings vii
3.1. Concordance Between Colorado DYS Strategic Plan Objectives
and Pilot Program 16
3.2. Summary of Qualitative Findings 19
3.3. Youth Demographic Characteristics 22
3.4. Proportion of Youth Experiencing Each Outcome by Unit 24
3.5. Adjusted Odds Ratios for Youth Outcomes for Pilot Unit 25
3.6. Educational Outcomes by Unit 25
3.7. Staff Absences and Turnover by Unit 26
3.8. Proportion of Staff Experiencing Each Outcome by Unit 26
3.9. Pilot Setup Costs 27
3.10. Running Costs Directly Attributable to the Pilot 29
A.1. Number of Incidents in Each Outcome Category Across Months 42
A.2. Mean Number of Outcomes per Youth by Unit 45
A.3. Adjusted Odds Ratios for Youth Outcomes for Pilot Unit ($n = 103$) 46
A.4. Number of Staff Leaving Unit per Month 46
C.1. LMYSC Facility-Wide Staff Costs (and FTEs), July 2018–June 2019 49
C.2. LMYSC Facility-Wide Other Labor Costs, July 2018–June 2019 50
C.3. LMYSC Facility-Wide Nonlabor Costs, July 2018–June 2019 50
C.4. Summary of Facility-Wide Running Costs and Corresponding Pilot Share,
July 2018–June 2019 51

Abbreviations

BHS   Behavioral Health Specialist

CI   confidence interval

DYS   Division of Youth Services

FTE   full-time equivalent

GEE   generalized estimating equation

HB   House Bill

LMYSC   Lookout Mountain Youth Services Center

MYSI   Missouri Youth Service Institute

OR   odds ratio

PREA   Prison Rape Elimination Act

YSS   Youth Services Specialist

CHAPTER ONE

Introduction

Youth involved in the juvenile justice system (including those who are arrested, detained, placed in juvenile facilities, and on community-based supervision) experience a number of challenges. A recent review found that 50–75 percent of youth involved in the juvenile justice system have mental health concerns, with mood disorders, attention-deficit/hyperactivity disorder, and posttraumatic stress disorder among the most prevalent diagnoses (Underwood and Washington, 2016). In addition, a substantial number of youth have trauma histories. A study of arrested and newly detained youth found that 93 percent had experienced at least one lifetime trauma, though the median number of traumas was a startling six incidents (Abram et al., 2004). Moreover, placement within the juvenile justice system can both exacerbate existing concerns and disrupt a youth's prosocial connections in the community. Particularly when confined in a residential facility, youth are removed from their support systems and enter an environment in which they are at risk for additional trauma and victimization (Ashkar and Kenny, 2008; Beck, Harrison, and Guerino, 2010; Dierkhising, Lane, and Natsuaki, 2013; Gatti, Tremblay, and Vitaro, 2009). Upon release, these youth remain at increased risk for lower educational achievement, reduced job prospects, requiring public assistance, and future delinquent behavior and incarceration (Beck, Harrison, and Guerino, 2010; DeLisi et al., 2011; Dmitrieva et al., 2012; Gilman, Hill, and Hawkins, 2015; Taylor, 1996). For this reason, the need for programs focused on rehabilitation—and for programs that are responsive to the specific issues faced by youth involved in the juvenile justice system—is substantial.

The juvenile justice system was designed to be a rehabilitative alternative to the adult criminal justice system (McCord, Spatz Widom, and Crowell, 2001). Over the past several decades, the extent to which the juvenile justice system has fulfilled its rehabilitative function has varied. For example, in the 1980s and 1990s, due to increasing concerns regarding serious offenses perpetrated by juveniles, the juvenile justice system became more punitive in nature (McCord, Spatz Widom, and Crowell, 2001). However, in recent years, the tide has begun to shift again (Underwood and Washington, 2016), and there has been an emphasis on rehabilitation—that is, providing programs that address individual needs to reduce future justice system contact (Andrews and Bonta, 2010). Despite this shift, there remain challenges to this goal. First, certain symptoms of mental health diagnoses can manifest as problem behaviors such as anger, irritability, and aggression (Underwood and Washington, 2016). Similarly, youth with a history of complex trauma may be at greater risk of exhibiting oppositional behavior, risk-taking, and poor impulse control (Ford et al., 2012). These types of behaviors can be challenging for staff members to address effectively, particularly when there are high youth to staff ratios, when staff are not sufficiently trained, or when the underlying mental health concerns are not treated. In addition, resources are often limited, which makes it challenging to effectively provide treatment services to youth in secure placement settings (Ramirez, 2008). In turn, this can lead to punitive practices, such as the use of restraints and seclusion. Though these efforts may be intended to control problem behaviors in the short term, these practices are a significant barrier to effective rehabilitation (Colorado Child Safety Coalition, 2017; Simkins, Beyer, and Geis, 2012). The use of punitive and physical practices not only prevents youth from feeling safe, but also has the potential to cause retraumatization (Colorado Child Safety Coalition, 2017).

As noted above, in recent years there have been efforts to realign juvenile justice systems with a more rehabilitative focus, and the state of Colorado is no exception. The Colorado Division of Youth Services (DYS) is the division of the Colorado Department of Human Services (CDHS) that provides care for youth committed by the District Court (CDHS, 2019b). DYS operates ten secure facilities and provides juvenile parole services for the state. For the past several years, DYS has implemented the Sanctuary Model (Bloom, 2005) across its facilities. Originally designed as a trauma-informed approach to inpatient treatment, the Sanctuary Model has been successfully implemented in other settings and populations, including juvenile justice-involved youth (Elwyn, Esaki, and Smith, 2015). The Sanctuary Model has its foundations in trauma theory and draws upon ten "tools," including supervision, training, team meetings, safety plans, and psychoeducation.

Despite the implementation of the Sanctuary Model, there were ongoing concerns about the safety of both youth and staff members within DYS. A report by the Colorado Child Safety Coalition (2017) covering the time period from 2013 to 2016 highlighted the use of punitive practices at DYS (at the time known as the Division of Youth Corrections) secure facilities, such as seclusion, restraints, and pain compliance techniques (i.e., placing pressure on nerve points). This report also documented increasing numbers of fights, assaults, and critical incidents, as well as injuries toward youth and staff members. In the report, staff members noted that they lacked training to appropriately de-escalate behavioral incidents. Together, as indicated in the report, these practices represented a significant barrier to effective rehabilitation.

In recognition of the challenges facing DYS, Colorado House Bill (HB) 17-1329 was introduced and signed into law in June 2017. This legislation sought to further promote a more rehabilitative culture within DYS. One key component of this statute was the creation of a pilot program within DYS using a therapeutic, group-treatment approach. The goal of this pilot program was to reduce the use of punitive practices, including seclusion and mechanical restraints; promote the physical and psychological safety of youth and staff; and, ultimately, to reduce recidivism. To accomplish these goals, the statute called for the pilot program to integrate trauma-responsive principles.

At the same time, Colorado DYS developed a Strategic Plan to guide its operation and programming. The Strategic Plan established the Colorado Model, which includes an explicit emphasis on establishing safe and trauma-responsive environments (see Figure 1.1). The Strategic Plan also established an Organizational Strategic Focus, identifying its goal as the following: "The Division will operate healthy trauma-responsive organizational environments as demonstrated through prosocial, safe and non-violent interactions." To achieve this goal, the Strategic Plan identified nine objectives that are consistent with principles of trauma-informed care, and which further shaped the establishment of the pilot program (see Box 1.1 for the complete list of Strategic Plan Objectives). These principles mirror the foundation of other programs designed to address trauma in juvenile justice facilities, such as the Missouri Model (Mendel, 2010), therapeutic communities (Kent, 2004), and units for youth with complex

Figure 1.1
The Colorado Model

Box 1.1: Colorado DYS Strategic Plan Objectives

1. Increase DYS senior leadership presence and engagement across the organization.
2. Create DYS small group processes to address day-to-day behavioral issues.
3. Shift the atmosphere of secure facilities to a more "homelike" atmosphere.
4. Create DYS "teams" of youth and staff in all facilities.
5. Optimize the use of residential state-operated and contract capacity.
6. Use the Behavioral Health framework to develop the DYS treatment approach.
7. Condense and simplify DYS staff training.
8. Trauma-responsive principles and practices will be integrated into all elements of the DYS organization.
9. Recruit, hire, and retain quality staff.

---

behavioral health needs (Ryan and Mitchell, 2011). Together with HB 17-1329, this Strategic Plan shaped the design and implementation of the trauma-informed pilot program at Lookout Mountain Youth Services Center (LMYSC).

Colorado DYS Pilot Program

LMYSC is one of two DYS secure facilities that exclusively serves committed youth (versus preadjudicated youth). It is designed to "treat the highest risk, highest need committed males" (CDHS, 2019b). LMYSC houses up to 140 male juvenile offenders and offers comprehensive services that are based on principles of cognitive behavioral therapy, social learning, and restorative community justice (CDHS, 2019b). The facility offers a range of programming to meet the needs of its youth, including academic programming, services focused on mental health and substance use concerns, and family programs (Colorado Office of Children, Youth & Families, 2019). LMYSC is organized into four units, one of which was selected to be transformed for the pilot program.

The pilot program was designed to be consistent with the Colorado Model. As required by HB 17-1329, key elements of the pilot program were to include a humane, homelike environment; to use small group processes to provide treatment; to avoid physical management and restraint; to phase out the use of certain restraint methods and seclusion completely within the first year of implementation; and to ensure staff were trained to provide trauma-responsive care. In turn, the goal of the pilot was to create an environment that is "safe, secure, and non-violent to promote building trust and healthy relationships between youths and staff and to allow youths to grow and mature responsibly."

To support the implementation of the pilot program, HB 17-1329 also called for the selection of an independent third party to serve as facilitators, coaches, and trainers. The Missouri Youth Service Institute (MYSI) was selected for this role. MYSI developed a model of trauma-informed care in the State of Missouri (often referred to as the Missouri Model). This trauma-informed approach to juvenile justice focuses on principles such as the use of small group processes, consistent youth supervision, problem-solving, family involvement, and reentry support (Mendel, 2010). Research suggests that this model is associated with reduced use of isolation, mechanical restraints, assaults on youth and staff, and property damage at juvenile justice facilities; improved educational progress while in custody; and ultimately reduced rates of recidivism following release (Mendel, 2010). Given the alignment between the principles and goals of the Missouri Model and the Colorado Model, Colorado DYS contracted with MYSI to employ two consultants during planning and implementation of the pilot program. The pilot program is described in more detail in subsequent chapters.

Present Evaluation

In addition to establishing the pilot program, HB 17-1329 required that the program be evaluated to assess its effectiveness during its first year of implementation. The goals of the evaluation included the following: (1) document the initial year of implementation of the pilot program, including the nature of the program, barriers and facilitators to implementation, and resources needed to sustain or expand the pilot program; (2) determine whether the pilot program was effective in reducing the number of negative incidents (e.g., fights, assaults, injuries, use of seclusion and restraints) and improving educational outcomes compared with a similar population of youth within DYS; (3) estimate the costs associated with implementation of the pilot program; and (4) develop recommendations to DYS regarding the pilot program, including any conclusions regarding scalability of the program. To achieve these goals, the RAND Corporation conducted a process and outcome evaluation of the pilot program, including conducting key stakeholder interviews regarding the nature of the pilot program, a document review, and a site visit. We conducted semistructured interviews with pilot program staff and collected administrative data on youth and staff outcomes from LMYSC for the pilot program and a comparison unit. We also conducted a cost analysis. In the next chapter, we describe the methodology in more detail.

CHAPTER TWO

Method

The evaluation focused on the first year of pilot program implementation (July 1, 2018, to June 30, 2019) and included a collection of primary data (observations during a site visit, document review, interviews) and secondary administrative data regarding youth and staff. The site visit and interviews were designed to examine the process of implementing the pilot program, whereas secondary data were designed to measure the short-term outcomes associated with the pilot program. All procedures were approved by the RAND Human Subjects Protection Committee and Colorado DYS.

Procedures

Key Informant Discussions, Document Review, and Site Visit

To better understand the nature of the pilot program, we completed a series of related procedures. First, we met with staff from DYS and LMYSC via telephone throughout the course of the project. We also had a discussion with one of the MYSI consultants regarding the nature of the training. The goal of these discussions was to understand the key elements of the pilot program, document the process of preparing for implementation and implementing the program, and understand any changes that took place over the course of the first year of implementation. There was no standard protocol for these discussions.

To supplement this, we also reviewed relevant program documents. This included HB 17-1329, the proposal that MYSI submitted to DYS for the training contract, the Colorado DYS Policy on Reporting Critical Incidents (CDHS, 2017a), the Colorado DYS Strategic Plan (CDHS, 2017b), and the MYSI Assessment of the Colorado Division of Youth Corrections (MYSI, 2017).

Finally, one project team member visited LMYSC in June 2019. The goal of this site visit was to meet with staff members and observe elements of the physical environment at LMYSC. Observational data collection during the site visit was largely informal, but the project team member did have an opportunity to examine differences in the rooms and common spaces for the pilot program compared with a traditional unit.

Qualitative Interviews

As part of the process evaluation, RAND conducted semistructured interviews with staff of the pilot program during the implementation year. The interview guide was developed using the Consolidated Framework for Implementation Research (CFIR) (Damschroder et al., 2009) and associated interview guide tool (CFIR Research Team, 2009), and was designed to be relevant to a range of staff members (including leadership, direct line staff, and behavioral health staff). Interview domains for all staff included background on the staff member and their role; nature of the pilot program; training and preparation; perceptions of the pilot program; barriers and challenges to implementation; and resources needed to sustain the pilot program (see Appendix B). Staff members in leadership positions were also asked questions about the process of preparing for implementation and considerations for evaluating the program. Interviews were approximately 30–45 minutes and were conducted by one member of the project team. All interviews took place in the last three months of the implementation year; some interviews took place via telephone, and others took place during the site visit. Detailed notes were taken during interviews and were used in analysis.

Administrative Data

For the outcome evaluation, administrative data regarding youth and staff were submitted to RAND by LMYSC on a monthly basis for the duration of the one-year evaluation period using an Excel data collection template developed by LMYSC and RAND staff. The outcomes of interest for the evaluation were specified within HB 17-1329, with an emphasis on examining whether there were reductions in negative outcomes (e.g., assaults, injuries, use of physical management). For this component of the evaluation, we collaborated with DYS and LMYSC staff to select another unit at LMYSC that would serve as a comparison group. We selected a comparison unit at LMYSC rather than another Colorado DYS facility because we expected that the implementation and outcomes associated with the pilot program would be influenced by facility-level policies and practices, and selecting a comparison group from a different facility may have introduced more variability with respect to these factors. Each unit at LMYSC is made up of multiple pods. The pilot unit was smaller than other units with regard to the number of pods and youth. Therefore, the comparison unit was selected based on size (i.e., identifying a unit with smaller pods) and on physical plant (i.e., having a building with a similar layout, as this relates to the way programming is provided at the facility). Because the pilot program unit included two pods, we obtained data from two pods in the comparison unit.

The unit selected to house the pilot program was originally designed to house youth with mental health concerns. Therefore, there may have been more youth with mental health concerns in the pilot group at the beginning of the evaluation. However, per facility and state policy, units at LMYSC are no longer filled based on specific youth characteristics. Therefore, any time there was a vacancy in any unit at the facility, the next youth needing a bed was moved into that vacancy. There was no systematic assignment to the comparison group versus pilot group during the evaluation period.

Of note, there were critical issues at the facility that took place in Spring 2019, including youth escapes and a riot, that resulted in the closing of the comparison unit on May 31, 2019. Therefore, our report of quantitative data focuses on the period of time from July 1, 2018, to May 31, 2019.

Youth Data

Data were submitted to RAND at the individual youth level on a monthly basis, and included the following information.

Demographic data and time at facility. Demographic data included age and race (black, white, or Hispanic). We also received data regarding date of entry to LMYSC, date of transfer to the pilot or comparison unit (as relevant), and date of discharge (as relevant). Using these data, we calculated the length of time that each youth spent on his respective unit during the evaluation period.

Committing offense. We received information about the nature of the committing offense for each youth, as identified in the Colorado DYS data system. These were classified into six categories: violent, sexual, property, firearm, drug, or "other" offenses.

Physical response. We received data regarding physical responses that took place during a given month. This included data about the measures used in the physical response (i.e., whether mechanical restraints were used or not), as well as the "level" of physical response based on Colorado DYS guidance. LMYSC provided data indicating whether a physical response included a mechanical restraint (e.g., handcuffs). They also reported on use of side holds, which is a technique used when a youth is handcuffed and becoming aggressive, such that staff members cradle the youth's head and shoulders into a side-lying position to prevent the youth from being in a prone position; as well as the use of transport restraints. Levels of physical responses were recorded using categories established by Colorado DYS. Level One refers to an "escort hold," in which a staff member holds a youth by the wrist and underarm to move him from one place to another, or a "standing torso hold," in which a staff member stands behind a youth who is fighting and puts their arms around the youth's torso to move him out of the way. Level Two refers to a range of approaches. It can include holding a youth on the ground in the prone position until they can be handcuffed, as well as a "team carry," which happens when a youth is resisting being held and presenting an emergency (e.g., by kicking and flailing against staff), and involves five staff members positioning themselves around the youth's body and carrying him a short distance. Finally, a "Critical" physical response is a self-defense response that a staff member can use only if he or she is being assaulted. It can include defense tactics such as grappling away from a youth, extending a forearm into a youth's chest, or extending a knee to the youth's inner thigh. We aggregated the number of incidents in each category for each youth across the study period. We also derived a dichotomous variable indicating whether a youth had experienced each of these physical responses during the study period (yes/no).

Seclusion. Data were submitted as to whether youth were secluded during a given month. Per HB 17-1329, any use of seclusion greater than four hours requires approval of the director of DYS. Therefore, use of seclusion was tracked in two categories: use of seclusion for less than four hours, and use of seclusion for four or more hours. We aggregated the number of uses of seclusion in each category across the study period. We also derived a dichotomous variable indicating whether a youth had experienced each length of seclusion during the study period (yes/no).

Fights and assaults. Data were provided as to whether youth were involved in any youth-on-youth fights or assaults, as well as any youth-on-staff fights or assaults. LMYSC classified these into four categories, which are used by Colorado DYS to characterize the nature of the fight or assault. Level One assaults are the result of an intentional act of aggression resulting in an injury that requires outside medical attention (e.g., stitches, an X-ray, concussion) that could not be addressed with first aid or a visit to the LMYSC medical provider. Level Two assaults are intentional acts of aggression resulting in injury that requires first aid or a visit to the LMYSC medical provider (e.g., for Steri-Strips or a Band-Aid). Level Three assaults are intentional acts of aggression resulting in injury that does not require first aid (e.g., resulting in a bruise; saliva that makes contact with the eyes or skin). "Unauthorized/Incidental" incidents reflect fights that are not the result of an intentional act of aggression.

Injuries. We received information as to whether a youth was injured during a given month. We aggregated the number of injuries per youth during the study period and derived a dichotomous variable indicating whether a youth had experienced an injury (yes/no).

Criminal charges filed. Data were provided as to any criminal charges filed against youth. We aggregated the number of times criminal charges were filed against each youth during the study period, and derived a dichotomous variable indicating whether a youth had any charges filed (yes/no).

Educational achievement. Data on educational achievement included the number of secondary credits earned at LMYSC during the evaluation year, as well as whether the youth earned his diploma or GED during the evaluation year. These outcomes were collected only for those youth who did not already have their degree at the beginning of the pilot program (note that there was one youth who had their GED at the beginning of the pilot but opted to continue earning credits to earn his diploma; this youth was retained for these analyses).

Staff Data

We also received data regarding staff of the pilot and comparison units. This included the following information.

Role at the facility. We received data on role at the facility, including whether the individual was a Youth Services Specialist (YSS), behavioral health staff, or social worker (these roles are described in more detail below). We also received information about the unit the staff member was assigned to for a given month.

Injuries. Data were provided as to whether each staff member experienced an injury in a given month (yes/no). These were aggregated into a single variable reflecting whether a staff member experienced an injury during the evaluation period.

Criminal charges and grievances/complaints. We received information as to whether criminal charges had been filed against a staff member (yes/no), which was aggregated into a single variable reflecting whether this took place at all during the evaluation period. We also received data regarding whether any grievances/complaints were made against an individual (yes/no), which was also aggregated into a single variable reflecting whether a staff member had a grievance/complaint filed against them during the study period.

Absences and turnover. We received information about the number of absences per month for each staff member and derived a variable reflecting the total number of absences during the study period. We also received information indicating whether a staff member left LMYSC during the evaluation period.

Cost Data

As the first step in the collection of cost data, we held preliminary conversations with representatives of DYS and LMYSC. These discussions revolved around two principal topics: (1) data collected by the DYS that could be made available to the research team; and (2) reflections of DYS and LMYSC representatives on costs incurred by the facility and, in particular, any unique costs incurred by the pilot. Based on these preliminary conversations, we developed a cost data template to be populated by the DYS. This template was based on past instruments used in other RAND projects (Hunt, Hunter, and Levan, 2017; Hunt, Ober, and Watkins, 2017), as well as tools developed by external organizations such as the cost module for the Substance Abuse Services Cost Analysis Program (Zarkin, Dunlap, and Homsi, 2004), and adapted to the needs and context of LMYSC. The template distinguished implementation and running costs and sought to collect data in the following categories: (1) personnel costs, (2) services, (3) facility costs, (4) equipment and supplies, and (5) other costs.

The draft cost data template was discussed with DYS representatives and further refined as necessary based on these conversations. DYS filled in the template with their financial data and shared the completed file with the research team. In addition, questions about costs were included in the topic guide used for the semistructured qualitative interviews. Their purpose was to collect stakeholder testimonies and insights that would offer additional context to the financial data and help with the interpretation of the data.

Data Analysis

Qualitative Interviews

To analyze the interview notes, we developed a structured codebook. Codes were initially created a priori based on the topics, subtopics, and concepts drawn from the interview guide. An inductive approach was used to augment the codebook with themes that emerged while conducting interviews and reviewing interview notes. Notes were coded and analyzed in Dedoose (SocioCultural Research Consultants, 2018), a qualitative data analysis software. Coding and analysis was conducted by a single project team member. Analysis included exploring the frequency of given codes and subcodes across the interviews to identify common themes emerging across interviews. Given the small number of staff members in the pilot program, we aggregated all responses together for analysis to mitigate the likelihood that staff members would be identifiable based on their responses. In our analysis, based on our coding guide, we focused on themes emerging in five key areas: (1) benefits to the pilot program, (2) drawbacks to the pilot program, (3) barriers to implementation, (4) proposed improvements to the pilot program and/or resources needed to sustain implementation, and (5) opportunities for improvement.

Administrative Data

To analyze the data, we first computed descriptive statistics regarding characteristics of the youth and staff in the pilot and comparison groups. For youth, this included age, race/ethnicity, and committing offense; for staff, this included role at the facility. We also examined whether there were differences in the mean length of time spent in each unit.

For youth, we then explored bivariate associations between unit and the mean number of incidents in each category described above, as well as the dichotomous indicator for each incident. These analyses revealed that on average, very few incidents in each category took place during the evaluation period. Given the rarity of these events, we focused on the dichotomous version of each outcome for subsequent analyses (Table A.2 lists the means for each outcome). We also examined bivariate associations between unit and each of the educational achievement variables. Next, we conducted a series of regression analyses to examine the effect of the unit (pilot versus comparison) on each outcome. These included logistic regression models for dichotomous outcomes and linear regression for continuous outcomes. All models controlled for length of time on the unit during the evaluation period, and models focused on educational outcomes also controlled for youth age.

For staff, we also began by exploring bivariate associations between unit and mean number of incidents in each category described above. We then conducted a series of analyses to examine the effect of the unit (pilot versus comparison) on each outcome, controlling for the number of months the staff member worked on the unit. Because there was a small number of staff members who worked on both units during the pilot, we used generalized estimating equation (GEE) binary logistic models for dichotomous outcomes and GEE linear models for continuous outcomes, which allowed us to account for those staff who worked both units.

As described above, there were several critical incidents that took place in Spring 2019. Combined with staffing challenges (described further in the results below), the facility made the decision to close one of the units on May 31, 2019, thereby reducing the overall census at the facility. The two pods in the comparison group were part of the closed unit. Therefore, our analysis of administrative data focuses on July 1, 2018, through May 31, 2019—that is, the first 11 months of implementation. Data were analyzed in SPSS (IBM Corporation, 2012) and R (R Core Team, 2017).

Cost Data

Data provided by DYS were processed and analyzed by the research team, with clarifications sought from DYS as necessary. The analysis of the cost data was undertaken with the objective to provide an overview of the following: (1) costs of setting up and operating the pilot as directly incurred by DYS, (2) comparison of pilot and nonpilot costs, (3) comparison of costs over time, and (4) unit costs (to the extent possible and analytically meaningful). Note that in the main text, we focus on summarizing the results of this analysis and provide more detailed results in Appendix C.

Evaluation Results

Description of the Pilot Program

As described above, one of the LMYSC units was selected to be transformed for the pilot program. This unit comprises two pods of 12 youth each, for a total of 24 youth on the unit. An overview of the timeline of pilot implementation appears in Figure 3.1. To better understand the nature of the pilot program at LMYSC, we engaged in discussions with key staff at DYS, LMYSC, and MYSI; conducted a review of documents from DYS; and conducted a site visit.

Staff and Staff Training

Our discussions with staff of DYS and LMYSC provided insight into staffing of the pilot program. The staffing levels for the pilot program are the same as those on other units at LMYSC, though HB 17-1329 explicitly notes that staffing of the program should be based on interest and preferences of the staff members. Staff included direct care staff, behavioral health providers, and unit and facility leadership. These included the following positions:

- **Youth Service Counselor III (YSCIII):** Units have a YSCIII, who serves as the unit manager. The unit manager provides supervision for the entire unit, including YSS staff and Behavioral Health Specialists (BHSs).
- **Youth Services Specialists (YSSs):** YSSs are responsible for implementing programming on the unit (e.g., daily groups, and "circle-ups" [see below]) as well as maintaining secu-

Figure 3.1
Timeline of Pilot Program Implementation

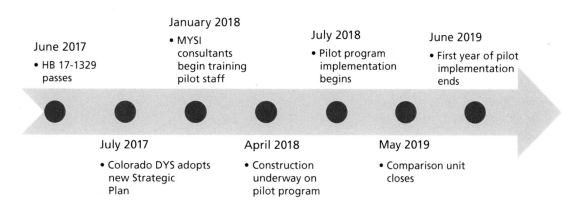

rity and safety. There were 15 YSS staff assigned to the pilot program at its initiation; during waking hours, the ratio of YSS staff to youth is no greater than 1:8, and during sleeping hours, the ratio is no greater than 1:16. The actual ratio could be lower than these figures, depending on the census of youth at the facility and available staff. Staffing ratios for the pilot program were consistent with required ratios across LMYSC units. YSS staff are designated at one of three levels:

- **YSSI and YSSII** staff members are direct care staff. They hold daily groups with youth and are responsible for much of the day-to-day milieu interactions.
- **YSSIII** staff members serve in supervisory positions. Units are designed to have two YSSIII staff, who generally have at least three years of supervisory experience and supervise the direct care staff.

At the beginning of the pilot program, the intention was that YSS staff would be specifically assigned to the pilot program; however, based on our key informant discussions, this became more difficult to maintain during the pilot implementation year due to staffing gaps on other units.

• **Behavioral Health Specialists (BHSs)**: There were three BHSs assigned to the pilot. Across the facility, these licensed master's-level clinicians carry a caseload of approximately eight youth and are responsible for conducting individual, family, and group therapy sessions. Individual and family sessions are held with youth from the unit to which BHSs are assigned (i.e., pilot program BHSs held these sessions with pilot program youth). As described below, group therapy sessions are specific to the types of offenses youth have committed, and therefore can include youth from multiple units.

One of DYS's goals is to increase leadership presence and engagement. Consistent with this objective, administrators had a role in the operation of the pilot program. First, a DYS-level administrator, the director of youth center operations, was hired to support the implementation of the pilot program. Facility-level and DYS-level administrators were also engaged in the pilot program through the Pilot Workgroup, which was led by the director of youth center operations and convened to give updates on the pilot program and discuss ideas for implementation. At the beginning of implementation, members of the Pilot Workgroup included facility-level leadership; the principal of the educational program at the facility; the pilot program unit manager; and four DYS-level administrators. The composition of the Pilot Workgroup evolved somewhat over time to include more representation from BHSs at the facility.

All LMYSC staff receive training in the Sanctuary Model, a trauma-informed model that has been implemented and evaluated for use with adjudicated youth (Elwyn, Esaki, and Smith, 2015; Peacock and Daniels, 2006); motivational interviewing; Verbal Judo, a communication approach designed to prevent conflicts from escalating (Verbal Judo Institute, Inc., n.d.); de-escalation skills; group processes; and adolescent development. For staff of the pilot program, this was supplemented by training from the MYSI consultants. Per our discussions with DYS and LMYSC staff, MYSI consultants supported the implementation of the pilot program in its first year, particularly with regard to small group processes, youth supervision, and family involvement in reentry support. For three months leading up to the opening of the pilot program, MYSI staff spent one week per month at LMYSC, during which time they provided a series of trainings on trauma-informed practices, following the Missouri Model. According to our discussions with a MYSI consultant, the training included ten modules and incorporated didactic elements and practical applications (e.g., case vignettes). The

Missouri Model training incorporates elements of existing models of leadership and group process (e.g., Tuckman Model of Group Development, Blanchard Situational Leadership Model) (Ken Blanchard Companies, 2019; Tuckman, 1965). It incorporates lessons related to the importance of understanding the roots of youth problem behavior, rather than focusing on the behaviors in isolation, including the role that previous trauma and experiences can play in driving youth behavior and reactions to situations. There are also modules dedicated to helping staff maintain professional boundaries and understand the role that their own history can play when working with youth and addressing problem behaviors. A primary goal of the training was to develop a positive, strong group culture on the pilot unit, including the philosophy that "we're not okay unless we're all okay."

According to the consultants and staff members, after the pilot program began on July 1, 2018, MYSI consultants spent three weeks per month at the pilot program throughout the first year of implementation to provide in-person coaching. This allowed them to continue to support program staff in implementation of the model, including hands-on assistance; on-site observation and modeling to staff; and ongoing consultation, feedback, and recommendations to facility and unit leadership. Per the consultant, an important element of the MYSI training and coaching is experiential learning. For example, if the consultants observed staff members handling a behavioral concern on the unit, their goal was to help staff to address the issue in real time and demonstrate how skills learned in training can be applied in practice. Our discussions with staff suggested that MYSI consultants largely served as observers during daytime programming, but would take notes, discuss observations with the unit manager, and occasionally provide guidance as to different ways to handle situations that arise.

Staff who joined the pilot program after July 2018 did not receive the same in-depth training as the original pilot staff. Originally, pilot program leadership noted that the plan was for the unit manager to provide new staff with this training in a "train-the-trainer" type model. However, our discussions revealed that this had not taken place. Therefore, new staff members did not receive the initial MYSI training, but did interact with the MYSI consultants on the unit.

Program Activities and Features

Through our discussions with DYS and LMYSC leadership, we learned about the pilot program activities and features. Of note, certain modifications were made to the program during its first year of implementation. To the extent possible, we highlight these changes or ways in which the program model differed from implementation.

Features of Programming Across LMYSC

Youth involved in the pilot program participated in many of the same activities as youth in other areas of the facility. In this section, we describe the core features of programming at LMYSC.

Youth at the facility attend school, which takes place from 8 a.m. to 2 p.m., Monday through Friday. Postsecondary education options are available as well, including culinary, construction trades, screen printing, hairstyling, and computer design. There is a recreation program, which includes physical education class at school and extracurricular recreation. Extracurricular recreation options include structured recreation within each pod, as well as the opportunity to participate in tournaments against other pods or other facilities.

Across the facility, small group activities are a core part of the program model. Pre/post groups are used to prepare youth for movements or schedule changes. For example, before a group moves to the central dining hall, they will convene as a group to remember what is needed and the expectations for movement. Other groups are implemented per the Sanctuary Model, such as problem-solving groups. Some of these groups also have shared features with the MYSI model. Therefore, though not all units at LMYSC are engaged in the pilot program, there are aspects of trauma-informed care present across the facility.

During their time at LMYSC, youth achieve different phase levels. Each of the phases has an associated workbook that youth complete, which includes various lessons. For example, the Welcome Phase addresses expectations at the facility; Phase 1 addresses themes such as nonviolence, emotional intelligence, and social learning; Phase 2 addresses themes such as loss and restorative community justice; and Phase 3 addresses themes such as values and goals, healthy relationships, and community resources. As youth complete the expectations for each phase, staff members working with the youth provide feedback about engagement in treatment, engagement in school, and behavior. To move on to the next phase, youth must complete a checklist of requirements, which include treatment assignments, feedback from staff, and completion of community service hours. Youth who have achieved the highest phase in the facility have access to the Eagles Program, in which they have access to additional amenities and privileges. For example, they have access to a lounge with additional games, movies, and treadmills, and can dial their own telephone calls. They can also go to other units to provide support to staff or other lower-phase youth.

All youth participate in regular behavioral health services. This includes three sessions per month with a BHS. Ideally, this would involve two individual and one family session, but if the family is unable to participate, it can be three individual sessions. In addition, youth receive at least one group therapy session per week. These treatment groups are determined based on the individual youth's treatment needs. For example, there are groups specific to the types of offenses youth have committed (e.g., groups for individuals who have committed sexual offenses or drug-related offenses). Youth often receive more than the required amount of session time per month; for example, youth currently receive two group sessions a week, and the facility plans to move to four group sessions a week. All youth in the Colorado DYS are assessed with a variety of clinical assessments including the Colorado Juvenile Risk Assessment (Colorado Department of Public Safety, 2019), University of California at Los Angeles Posttraumatic Stress Disorder Reaction Index (Steinberg et al., 2004), and Juvenile Assessment and Intervention System (JAIS) (National Council on Crime and Delinquency, 2019). If a specific need emerges based on an assessment, a youth may be assigned to an additional group or service.

Features Specific to the Pilot Program

According to our discussions, prior to the implementation of the pilot program LMYSC units housed youth based on type of offense or specific treatment needs. The unit selected to house the pilot program was originally designed to house youth with mental health concerns. However, per our discussions, LMYSC has moved away from this model. Therefore, while youth at the beginning of the program may have had more needs related to mental health, new youth who entered during the course of the implementation year were not selected based on any specific characteristics (i.e., the next youth needing a bed at a facility was moved into a vacancy when it became available).

The pilot program builds upon traditional programming from the time that youth enters the facility. First, the pilot program was designed to include a specific set of orientation activities. In addition to providing a welcome bag to youth upon entry, youth participate in a welcome group and are paired with a peer mentor and staff person. The staff person not only helps orient the youth, but also stays in contact with the parents to inform them about the program.

The pilot program aimed to create a more homelike environment for youth. To accomplish this, the pilot unit underwent a significant renovation prior to implementation. Though the unit has an identical footprint to other units at LMYSC, the pilot program uses less institutional furniture, bigger mattresses, and traditional comforters. Paint colors were changed to be less institutional. During a site visit to LMYSC, these physical differences between the pilot program unit and other units at the facility were clear. One of the MYSI consultants also reported that he encourages staff to display youth achievements and artwork, and to incorporate aspects of the treatment philosophy (e.g., charts with different emotions, community standards). In addition, youth in the pilot program were given access to more amenities (e.g., name-brand toiletries) and normal adolescent activities (e.g., radios, video games, puzzles, coloring books).

A critical aspect of the pilot program is the importance of the community and the small group process. As noted, the pilot program comprised 24 youth who are divided into two smaller groups based on their housing pod (i.e., there are two pods within the pilot program unit). The pilot program aimed to keep youth with other members of their group as much as possible throughout the day. These small groups met daily and participated in other treatment-related activities together. Though pilot youth are with other youth for academic time, the pilot youth are kept together for homeroom class and for physical education. Certain elements of the Missouri Model have also been incorporated to address issues that arise, including behavioral concerns. These include "circle-ups," which are spontaneous groups convened to address a specific incident or conflict that has occurred. The goal is to promote honest and open discussion and engage in problem-solving. Staff were also encouraged to implement check-in/processing sessions, which are daily meetings that bring together the group to check in about how they are feeling, both individually and as a group. These sessions can be used to process a specific task or event as needed. Through these mechanisms, when youth engage in problematic behavior, staff are meant to encourage them to take accountability and receive feedback from their peers. Weekly group meetings were also held to discuss any positive or negative things taking place in the pod. Combined with the DYS behavior expectations, which focus on forming a community of dignity and respect, the goal is to promote a therapeutic milieu in which youth feel safe and more comfortable disclosing concerns. Ultimately, this creates the opportunity to provide treatment and address youth needs.

When the pilot program was created, staff also planned for additional programming that was unique to the pilot program. For example, a yoga class was implemented for a period of time, and the staff on the unit has started a running club for youth. However, these additional programs are largely based on interest and availability of staff members.

Parental engagement is a key element of the Colorado Model. Though family members of youth at LMYSC are often engaged already, the pilot program developed an enhanced aftercare component to further serve youth and their families. Through the aftercare component, a licensed master's-level clinician would offer family therapy to youth and families 90 days prior to parole, and continue providing this service for 90 days after parole in the family's own community. The goal of this component is to help understand and address any issues that the family has and connect them with resources that they may need. Though this was initially intended to be an element of the program model, discussions with staff indicated that it was not possible to fully offer this element during the first year of implementation. However, family participation was encouraged in other ways. For example, the program held regular family engagement events where parents were able to participate in engaging and developmentally focused activities with their youth on campus.

Concordance Between Colorado DYS Strategic Plan Objectives and Pilot Program Features

The pilot program was designed in part to be consistent with the Strategic Plan Objectives established by DYS, as these objectives were established to create a trauma-responsive environment across DYS. In Table 3.1, we summarize features of the pilot program that pertain to each of these objectives.

Pilot Program Logic Model

Based on the information gathered about the pilot program, we developed the logic model in Figure 3.2. The first column summarizes the resources and inputs needed to operate the pilot program, including staff, training, facilities, collaborations, and other resources. The second

Table 3.1
Concordance Between Colorado DYS Strategic Plan Objectives and Pilot Program

Strategic Plan Objective	Pilot Program Features
Increase DYS Senior Leadership presence and engagement across the organization	• DYS and LMYSC administrators have a role in the operation of the pilot program, including through the Pilot Workgroup
Create DYS small group processes to address day-to-day behavioral issues	• The pilot program includes two small groups of 12 youth, and aims to keep youth with other members of their group throughout the day
	• Group meetings (e.g., circle-ups, check-in/processing sessions) are used to address behavioral problems
Shift the atmosphere of secure facilities to a more "homelike" atmosphere	• The pilot program has less institutional furniture, more comfortable bedding, less institutional paint colors
Create DYS "teams" of youth and staff in all facilities	• Youth are paired with peer mentors upon entry to the facility
	• Youth are kept with other members of their pod through as much programming as possible
Optimize the use of residential state-operated and contract capacity	(Not evaluated)
Use the Behavioral Health framework to develop the DYS treatment approach	• All youth participate in regular behavioral health services, consistent with the broader LMYSC community
Condense and simplify DYS staff training	• All LMYSC staff are provided with training in the Sanctuary Model; pilot staff received additional intensive training in the months leading up to pilot implementation
Trauma-responsive principles and practices will be integrated into all elements of the DYS organization	• The pilot program is explicitly predicated on principles of trauma-informed care, with additional support and training provided by consultants from MYSI
Recruit, hire, and retain quality staff	• All pilot program staff at the beginning of the program participated in training to ensure they had needed skills

Figure 3.2
Pilot Program Logic Model

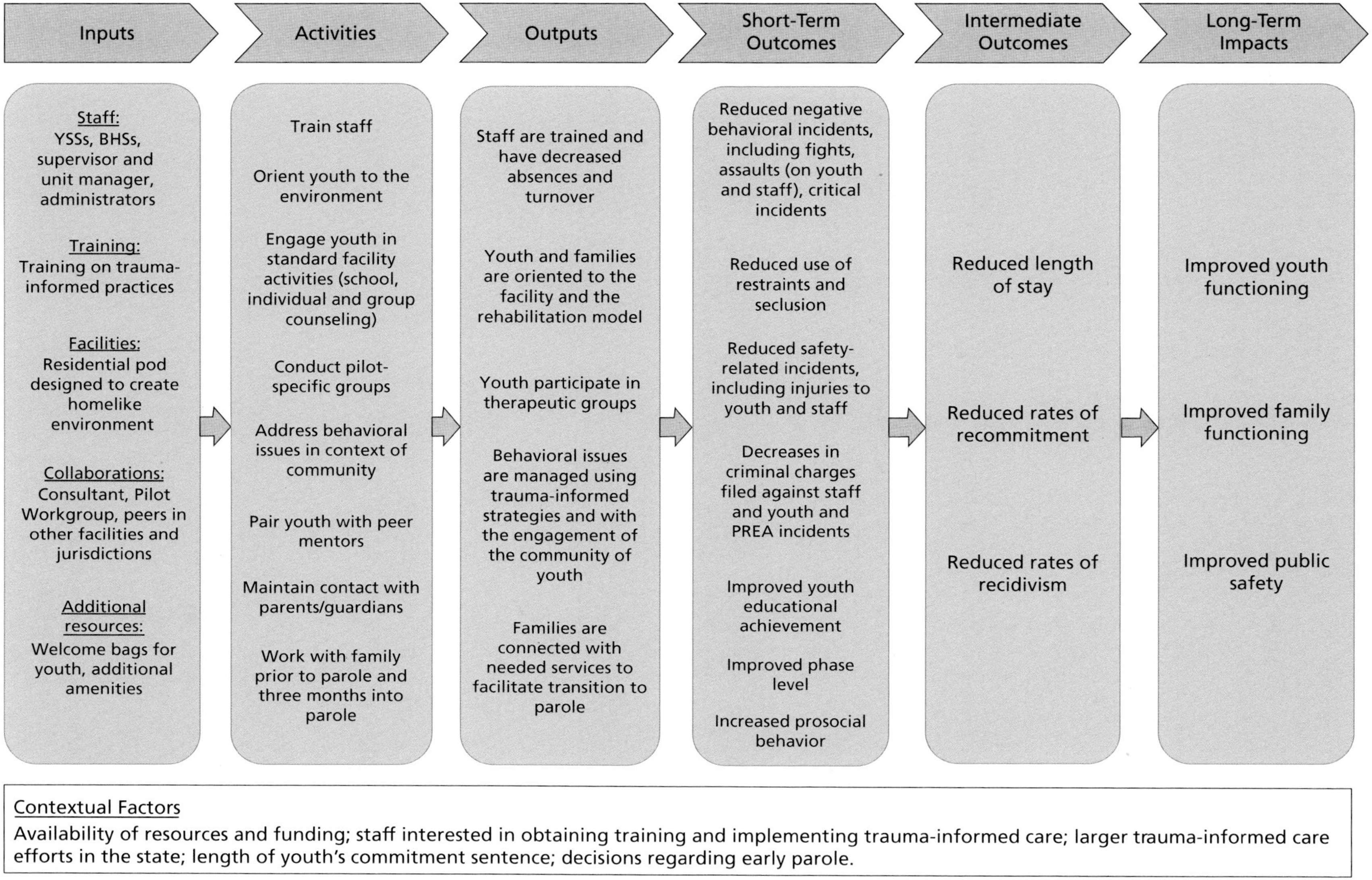

Inputs	Activities	Outputs	Short-Term Outcomes	Intermediate Outcomes	Long-Term Impacts
Staff: YSSs, BHSs, supervisor and unit manager, administrators	Train staff	Staff are trained and have decreased absences and turnover	Reduced negative behavioral incidents, including fights, assaults (on youth and staff), critical incidents	Reduced length of stay	Improved youth functioning
Training: Training on trauma-informed practices	Orient youth to the environment	Youth and families are oriented to the facility and the rehabilitation model	Reduced use of restraints and seclusion	Reduced rates of recommitment	Improved family functioning
Facilities: Residential pod designed to create homelike environment	Engage youth in standard facility activities (school, individual and group counseling)	Youth participate in therapeutic groups	Reduced safety-related incidents, including injuries to youth and staff	Reduced rates of recidivism	Improved public safety
Collaborations: Consultant, Pilot Workgroup, peers in other facilities and jurisdictions	Conduct pilot-specific groups	Behavioral issues are managed using trauma-informed strategies and with the engagement of the community of youth	Decreases in criminal charges filed against staff and youth and PREA incidents		
Additional resources: Welcome bags for youth, additional amenities	Address behavioral issues in context of community	Families are connected with needed services to facilitate transition to parole	Improved youth educational achievement		
	Pair youth with peer mentors		Improved phase level		
	Maintain contact with parents/guardians		Increased prosocial behavior		
	Work with family prior to parole and three months into parole				

Contextual Factors

Availability of resources and funding; staff interested in obtaining training and implementing trauma-informed care; larger trauma-informed care efforts in the state; length of youth's commitment sentence; decisions regarding early parole.

column summarizes the pilot program activities, including the staff training and core features of the program described above. The third column highlights the outputs anticipated from these activities (e.g., youth participation in programming, management of behavioral issues).

The last three columns summarize the outcomes expected from the program. In the short term, the pilot program is expected to decrease negative behavioral incidents, reduce use of restraints and seclusion as behavior management techniques, decrease injuries, decrease criminal charges filed, improve youth educational achievement, and improve phase level. With regard to intermediate outcomes, the program is expected to reduce length of stay at the facility, as youth may be seen as ready for parole more quickly; reduce rates of recommitment; and reduce rates of recidivism. Ultimately, these outcomes are expected to result in improved youth and family functioning, as well as improved public safety.

Qualitative Findings Regarding Program Implementation

A subset of ten staff members participated in qualitative interviews, which provided critical information about the process of implementing the pilot program. A range of staff participated in these interviews, including direct-line staff (YSS staff), BHS staff, and leadership. The main themes that emerged are described below and summarized in Table 3.2.

Benefits of the Pilot Program

The most commonly identified benefit of the pilot program was improved relationships between youth and staff. Interviewees described how they worked to build relationships with the youth and identify their needs. When behavioral problems arise, having a well-established relationship with the youth allows staff to focus on problem-solving rather than punishment. One staff member noted that she appreciates "sitting down with [youth] and talking to them instead of being authoritarian." Another staff member highlighted that with the shift to this relationship-based approach, youth seem more receptive to staff messages.

Staff members also highlighted the additional amenities available to youth, including renovated rooms and newer furniture; better hygiene items; and access to more typical youth activities such as video games, AM/FM radios, and games, which "promote normalcy."

Drawbacks to the Pilot Program

Though staff acknowledged that the pilot program has provided them with new ways to approach behavioral issues, the most commonly described drawback to the pilot program was a perceived lack of behavior management tools. For example, one staff member described being inadvertently tackled when trying to break up a fight between youth. In this situation, as the staff member said, "Unless they come at me directly, there's nothing I can do about it. This unit doesn't have seclusion at all. We can keep them in cuffs until they're calm, but that's it." This was a situation in which the staff member wished there were more "repercussions" to youth actions. Another staff member noted that youth can be disrespectful or engage in problematic behavior with no consequences, and wondered if that was indirectly "rewarding" the youth. Finally, one staff member acknowledged that eliminating seclusion is beneficial, in that seclusion can be traumatizing. However, this staff member described the value of "containment" in more extreme situations (e.g., "causing physical harm every day"), noting that this was no longer an option.

Table 3.2
Summary of Qualitative Findings

Category	Common Themes
Benefits of the pilot program	• Positive relationships between youth and staff • Ability to use relationship to manage behavioral concerns • Amenities for youth that promote normalcy
Drawbacks to the pilot program	• Limited behavioral management tools for more extreme situations (e.g., fights, assaults) • Safety concerns • Animosity from staff and youth from other units
Barriers to implementation	• Short-staffed at facility and high levels of turnover • Different training for newer pilot program staff and insufficient levels of training • Facility-level issues (e.g., riot) • Difficulty reconciling state and facility policies with need to manage problematic behavior
Facilitators of implementation	• Initial pilot training and MYSI consultants • Leadership support and relationships among staff members
Resources needed	• Additional training, including training more tailored to different staff roles • Additional staff members with relevant experience or education
Opportunities for improvement	• Keep youth from pilot together as much as possible • Additional programs (e.g., recreational options) • Incorporation of other evidence-based practices

In turn, about half the staff members interviewed described safety concerns. As one interviewee stated, "We have staff getting verbally and physically beat up." Staff members reported that they and their colleagues no longer feel safe, and indicated that this is a recent change. It is important to note that this may not be a problem unique to the pilot program, but could also reflect some larger policy changes in DYS (described below). As a result of these safety concerns, though, there has been substantial turnover at the facility.

Finally, a small number of staff members reported that they have experienced some animosity from staff and youth on other units. They noted that a perception on the part of both staff and youth on other units was that in the pilot program, "youth get what they want."

Barriers to Implementation

During the interviews, a number of barriers to implementation were raised. The most commonly identified barrier to implementation was staffing at the facility. Almost all interviewees described how the facility has been short-staffed, which has made it difficult to implement the program as intended. They noted that staffing first became a problem in fall 2018, as there was a scheduling change. As a result of the scheduling change, many people left the facility. In addition, they described high levels of turnover resulting from staff members feeling unsafe.

In turn, being short-staffed has resulted in multiple challenges to implementation. First, interviewees described how one foundational tenet of the pilot program is having consistency in staff and fostering relationships between staff and youth. Because there are many new staff members, it has been hard to foster these relationships. Second, as noted above, only staff who were at the facility at the beginning of the implementation period received the initial intensive training from the MYSI consultants. Therefore, newer program staff have received less training in the model, and, as one interviewee noted, this is resulting in "disagreement in what trauma-informed care looks like." In addition, because other units may also be short-staffed, even those pilot program staff who have been trained sometimes get pulled to cover other units.

A related category of barriers was facility-level issues. Discussions with staff highlighted several issues that took place during the evaluation period, including youth escapes and a significant riot on the comparison unit, which ultimately resulted in the closure of the unit. These facility-level issues resulted in downstream effects on the pilot. For example, staff members reported that when the unit closed following the riot (May 2019), several youth were transferred to the pilot program, which disrupted the relationships that had already been formed between youth and staff. In addition, another interviewee noted that when there are major safety concerns (e.g., rumor of a gun on campus), the campus will implement highly structured programming, which prevents the pilot program from implementing activities as usual. Finally, as stated, being short-staffed in other areas of the facility affects staffing levels on the pilot unit.

Another common barrier to implementation was staff perceptions of facility- and state-level policies. A recent policy change eliminated strip searches of youth at the facility as part of the larger effort within DYS to implement a trauma-informed model. Staff members reported that this has increased the presence of drugs and contraband at the facility. One staff member noted that "a lot of youth are using drugs," which has changed the dynamic of groups held on the unit because "the youth don't want to engage." Other staff members highlighted differences between Colorado state policies and those in other states implementing similar models. In particular, they described difficulty implementing some of the suggestions from the MYSI consultants because of these differences. For example, as one staff member said, "There are different repercussions that kids have out there [in Missouri] that they don't have here. If you do attack a staff member, you're off the facility [and] going to the jail system. Here, it's a little different. If you attack a staff, we'll do what we have to do, use community restoring techniques." When asked if these techniques were effective, the staff member said, "With certain youth. Then certain youth care less." Of note, these policies would not necessarily affect just the pilot program. However, these differences in state policies were perceived as limiting the extent to which the MYSI consultants could help staff to navigate some of these difficult or extreme situations.

Finally, staff cited a lack of training as a barrier to implementation. In part, this related to the fact that newer staff did not receive the initial MYSI training. One staff member said that they had made requests for more training, but it had not resulted in changes. Another staff member highlighted that the low staffing levels made it difficult to provide needed training.

As a result of these barriers, staff members noted that they had not fully been able to implement the pilot program. As one staff member said, "Though you still have problems in the pilot, you don't have the same extremes as you do in the other units. I think it was a good first year. I'm glad it will continue for the next year because we learned about what worked well and ways you really can impact the kids. But just based on the chaos of the campus [i.e., the larger facility], I don't know if it got a full chance."

Facilitators of Implementation and Resources Needed

When asked about facilitators of implementation, a small number of staff members described the usefulness of training, including the ongoing consultation of the MYSI consultants, as well as leadership support, including support from the unit manager, as well as support from DYS administrators, facility administrators, and the Pilot Workgroup. A small number of staff members also highlighted the importance of relationships among the staff members. For example, one interviewee stated, "This unit has had such a good balance of working with the therapists and the line staff. . . . We coincide very well together, they both respect each other, and other units struggle with that immensely."

Perhaps unsurprisingly, additional staff and training were highlighted as resources needed to improve and/or sustain the implementation of the pilot program. Regarding training, one interviewee suggested that "step one" would be training on "safety and how safety builds into a trauma-informed environment." Others suggested that the MYSI consultants could work closely with new staff to provide more one-on-one coaching, and could do more modeling of skills for staff members. Another interviewee suggested that training other, nonpilot staff members would help to establish the pilot program model across the facility. It is important to note that staff expressed varying perceptions of the initial MYSI training received. Whereas some found it helpful and engaging, those with more of a background in trauma-informed care found it less useful. The latter group suggested there could be ways to dive deeper into the content and spend more time discussing application of the information. Similarly, some staff reported benefiting from the ongoing presence of the MYSI consultants, noting that they are able to give pointers and model skills in the moment; however, others said they perceived the consultants as more passive observers.

Regarding staff, interviewees highlighted the need to recruit and retain staff at all levels. As one interviewee said, "More people will promote safety." They also highlighted the need for consistency in staff. Some interviewees noted that better benefits or salary might help in recruitment and retention of staff, and one interviewee emphasized the importance of recruiting high-quality staff with relevant backgrounds.

Opportunities for Improvement

About half of the staff interviewed described new programming that would improve the pilot program. For example, currently youth attend behavioral health and offense-specific groups with youth from other units. Some staff members suggested it would be beneficial to keep all groups within the pilot unit so that youth could stay together for most of their programming, which is an element of the Missouri Model. Though this would require additional staff, the amount of time needed would be minimal, approximately "1 or 2 people a couple times a week." Other staff suggested additional small group activities that would keep youth "busy in a healthy way." Specific ideas included a running club, horticulture club, reading club, and poetry club. Staff members noted that these types of activities "could fill structured leisure time," and would "promot[e] the relationships, the growth, talking about selves without realizing [it]. Learning basic life skills, social skills." Finally, one staff member suggested incorporating music therapy or art therapy.

A handful of other ideas for improvement were suggested. For example, one staff member suggested the implementation of additional evidence-based practices, such as the risk-need-responsivity model, through which specific services and the intensity of those services would be tailored to the risk level and need of individual youth (Bonta and Andrews, 2017). Some suggested finding ways to promote communication across staff members and ensure staff members are "on the same page." Finally, one staff member highlighted the need to value employee engagement and increase recognition of employees.

Youth Program Outcomes

In this section, we summarize the results of quantitative analyses of administrative data regarding youth in the study. Administrative data were collected on youth who resided on the pilot or comparison units during the evaluation period. This included youth who were on these units at the beginning of the evaluation period, as well as youth who entered these units during the year of implementation. There were 24 youth in the pilot group at the beginning of the pilot year and 40 youth in the comparison group. During the pilot year, 29 youth were discharged from the pilot and 35 youth were discharged from the comparison. In total, data were collected on 48 pilot youth and 68 comparison youth.

We began the quantitative analysis by comparing the demographic characteristics of youth in the pilot and comparison groups; the results are summarized in Table 3.3. There were no significant differences between the groups with respect to age, race/ethnicity, time spent on unit, or committing offense.

On average, youth on the pilot unit spent a little more than five months on the unit during the evaluation period (median = 170.50 days, interquartile range = 50.00, 243.25). Of the 24 youth who were on the pilot unit at the beginning of the evaluation period (July 1, 2018),

Table 3.3
Youth Demographic Characteristics

Demographics	Pilot (*n* = 48) M (SD) or % (*n*)	Comparison (*n* = 68) M (SD) or % (*n*)
Age at entry (years)	17.65 (1.34)	17.69 (1.33)
Race/ethnicity		
Black	27.1% (13)	32.8% (22)
White	37.5% (18)	31.3% (21)
Hispanic	35.4% (17)	35.8% (24)
Time spent on unit (days)	167.7 (16.4)	159.7 (12.6)
Committing offense type		
Drug	0.0% (0)	3.4% (2)
Firearm	11.4% (5)	18.6% (11)
Property	11.4% (5)	22.0% (13)
Sexual	20.5% (9)	13.6% (8)
Violent	54.5% (24)	35.6% (21)
Other	2.3% (1)	6.8% (4)
Committing offense degree		
Misdemeanor	28.6% (12)	36.8% (21)
Felony	71.4% (30)	63.2% (36)

the average length of stay at the facility was 18.7 months, of which 7.3 months was during the evaluation period. Those who entered the pilot during the evaluation period were on the unit for an average of 3.8 months before the end of the evaluation period (May 31, 2019).

Regarding the comparison unit, on average, youth also spent a little more than five months on the unit during the evaluation period (median = 138.50 days, interquartile range = 60.25, 243.25). Of the 40 youth who were on the comparison unit at the beginning of the evaluation period, the average length of stay was 16.2 months, of which 5.6 months was during the evaluation period. Those youth who entered the comparison unit during the evaluation period had an average length of stay of 4.9 months before the end of the evaluation period.

Taken together, these data suggest that youth on the pilot unit had been at the facility somewhat longer than those in the comparison unit at the time the pilot program began. However, these variances were not significantly different.

Impact of Program on Negative Youth-Related Outcomes

Across the evaluation period, physical responses with mechanical restraints and Level Two physical responses were most common. Of note, the maximum number of physical responses with mechanical restraints or Level Two physical responses for a given youth in any month was seven incidents. On both units, most outcomes were fairly evenly spread across each month of the implementation year. There are two notable exceptions to this. First, the number of youth injuries spiked on both units during April and May. Second, during the month of February, nine pilot youth had criminal charges filed (see Table A.1 for a summary of the total number of incidents occurring on each unit during each month of the evaluation period).

Descriptive statistics for each of the negative outcomes of interest are summarized in Table 3.4. As described, when examined at the youth level, the mean number of each type of incident per youth was very low for most outcomes; therefore, we focus on reporting the proportion of youth in each unit who experienced each outcome during the study period. For a table reporting the mean number of each outcomes experienced by each youth, see Table A.2.

The proportion of youth experiencing each outcome was not significantly different for most categories. However, significantly fewer pilot youth experienced physical responses with mechanical restraints (44.9 percent) or Level Two physical responses (44.9 percent) than comparison youth (69.1 percent and 67.7 percent, respectively). However, a greater proportion of pilot youth experienced a side hold (14.3 percent) than comparison youth (0.0 percent). In addition, significantly more pilot youth had criminal charges filed (22.4 percent compared with 1.4 percent of comparison youth).

In addition to bivariate associations between unit and each outcome, we conducted a series of logistic regression analyses to examine the effect of the unit, controlling for youth length of time on each unit. Note that it was not possible to include all outcomes in these regression analyses; specifically, we did not conduct regressions for outcomes that did not occur in either unit (e.g., Level Three and Critical physical responses); nor for outcomes with a zero value for one of the units (e.g., there were no Level One youth on staff assaults in the comparison group during the study period), which were generally rare outcomes on both units. Results are summarized in Table 3.5. Significant effects were observed for three outcomes. Youth on the pilot unit were significantly less likely to have experienced a physical response with mechanical restraints or a Level Two physical response. However, they were significantly more likely to have had criminal charges filed. As indicated above, this difference appears to be entirely due to events in a single month (February), during which nine pilot youth had criminal charges filed.

Table 3.4
Proportion of Youth Experiencing Each Outcome by Unit

Outcomes	Pilot % (n)	Comparison % (n)	p-value
Physical Response			
Without mechanical restraint	20.8% (10)	26.5% (18)	p=0.49
With mechanical restraint	45.8% (22)	69.1% (47)	p=0.01*
Side hold	10.4% (5)	0.0% (0)	p=0.01*
Transport restraint	0.0% (0)	0.0% (0)	N/A
Level One	18.8% (9)	25.0% (17)	p=0.43
Level Two	45.8% (22)	67.6% (46)	p=0.02*
Critical	0.0% (0)	0.0% (0)	N/A
Seclusion			
Seclusion < 4 hours	16.7% (8)	13.2% (9)	p=0.61
Seclusion 4+ hours	0.0% (0)	0.0% (0)	N/A
Assaults/fights—youth on youth			
Unauthorized/incidental	33.3% (16)	42.6% (29)	p=0.31
Level One	0.0% (0)	4.4% (3)	p=0.26
Level Two	14.6% (7)	7.4% (5)	p=0.23
Level Three	22.9% (11)	19.1% (13)	p=0.62
Assaults/fights—youth on staff			
Unauthorized/Incidental	0.0% (0)	0.0% (0)	N/A
Level One	4.2% (2)	0.0% (0)	p=0.17
Level Two	6.3% (3)	1.5% (1)	p=0.31
Level Three	6.3% (3)	4.4% (3)	p=0.69
Youth Injuries			
Injuries	29.2% (14)	23.5% (16)	p=0.50
Charges Filed			
Criminal charges filed	22.9% (11)	1.5% (1)	p<0.001**

*p<0.05, **p<0.01

We also examined models that controlled for youth committing offense type, and the results were largely similar, though the effect of the unit on Level Two physical responses became marginally significant. Because youth committing offense was only available for 103 of the youth, we report these results in Appendix A (Table A.3).

Impact of Program on Educational Outcomes

We also examined the effect of the program on youth educational outcomes. There was no significant difference in the proportion of youth in each group who arrived at the facility with a degree (either high school diploma or GED). Data were available for 114 of the youth. Approximately 34 percent (n = 16) of pilot youth and 39 percent (n = 26) of comparison youth already had their degree at the beginning of the pilot program.

Table 3.5
Adjusted Odds Ratios for Youth Outcomes for Pilot Unit

Outcome	OR (95% CI)[a]
Physical Response	
Without mechanical restraint	0.69 (0.28, 1.71)
With mechanical restraint	0.35 (0.16, 0.77)**
Level One	0.64 (0.25, 1.63)
Level Two	0.38 (0.17, 0.82)*
Seclusion	
Seclusion <4 hours	1.21 (0.41, 3.60)
Assaults/Fights—Youth on Youth	
Unauthorized/Incidental	0.62 (0.28, 1.38)
Level Two	2.09 (0.62, 7.11)
Level Three	1.22 (0.49, 3.06)
Assaults/Fights—Youth on Staff	
Level Two	4.50 (0.45, 44.73)
Level Three	1.36 (0.26, 7.18)
Injuries	
Injuries	1.33 (0.57, 3.07)
Charges Filed	
Criminal charges filed	22.27 (2.64, 187.93)**

NOTE: Comparison unit is the referent for analyses.
*p<0.05, **p<0.01
[a] Odds ratios (OR) are adjusted for youth length of stay on the unit.
CI = confidence interval.

Table 3.6
Educational Outcomes by Unit

Educational Outcome	Pilot % (n) or M (SD)	Comparison % (n) or M (SD)	p-value
Number of credits earned	39.11 (23.80)	40.20 (26.64)	p=0.86
Diploma or GED earned	29.0% (9)	22.0% (9)	p=0.49

Within the subset of youth who had not yet earned their degree ($n = 41$ pilot youth, $n = 31$ comparison youth), we examined the mean number of credits earned during the pilot year. We also examined the proportion of youth per unit who earned a diploma or GED. There was no significant difference for either outcome (see Table 3.6).

Because both outcomes had the potential to be influenced by youth age and time spent on a given unit during the pilot year, we conducted regression analyses to control for these variables. In these models, there was still no significant effect of the unit on the number of credits earned ($b = -2.98$, standard error = 4.79, p = 0.54) or likelihood of earning a diploma or GED (OR = 1.35; 95 percent CI: 0.41, 4.39; p = 0.62).

Staff Outcomes

In this section, we summarize the results of quantitative analyses of administrative data regarding staff. Administrative data were collected on staff who worked on the pilot or comparison units during the evaluation period. This included staff who were on these units at the beginning of the evaluation period, as well as new staff who began working on these units during the evaluation period. In total, data were collected on 45 pilot staff and 64 comparison staff from July 1, 2018, to May 31, 2019.

Differences Between Units on Absences and Turnover

We first examined differences by unit with respect to absences and turnover. The number of absences per staff member ranged widely from 0 to 156 days during the study period. Therefore, we also computed the mean number of absences per month to account for the different lengths of time that staff were on each unit. Absences per month ranged from 0 to 23 days. The average total number of absences per staff and absences per month is reported in Table 3.7, as well as the proportion of staff who left the facility. There were no significant differences between units for these measures. Table A.4 summarizes the number of staff members from each unit who left the facility for each month of the evaluation period.

In addition, we examined whether there were any differences between the pilot and comparison unit with respect to absences and turnover, controlling for length of time working on the unit during the evaluation period. Three staff members worked on both units during the reporting period. Therefore, we used GEE models to account for these staff members. There was still no significant effect of the unit on absences ($b = 0.74$, SE = 3.45, p = 0.83) or turnover (OR = 1.19; 95 percent CI: 0.50, 2.83; p = 0.69).

Impact of Program on Negative Staff-Related Outcomes

Regarding staff outcomes, we examined whether a staff member had experienced a given outcome during the pilot period (Table 3.8). There was no significant difference in the proportion

Table 3.7
Staff Absences and Turnover by Unit

Outcome	Pilot M (SD) or % (n)	Comparison M (SD) or % (n)	p-value
Total absences (days)	17.4 (27.14)	15.38 (17.50)	p = 0.64
Absences per month (days)	2.68 (2.81)	3.14 (3.80)	p = 0.49
Staff left facility	31.10% (14)	29.70% (19)	p = 0.87

Table 3.8
Proportion of Staff Experiencing Each Outcome by Unit

Outcome	Pilot % (n)	Comparison % (n)	p-value
Staff injuries	15.6% (7)	23.4% (15)	p = 0.31
Grievances/complaints filed	0.0% (0)	0.0% (0)	N/A
Criminal charges filed	0.0% (0)	0.0% (0)	N/A

of staff who were injured on each unit. Of note, there were no staff who had grievances/complaints or criminal charges filed against them during the study period.

We also used a GEE model to examine the effect of the unit on staff injuries, controlling for length of time on the unit. The effect of the unit remained nonsignificant (OR = 0.54; 95 percent CI: 0.18, 1.62; p = 0.28).

Cost Analysis

This section discusses the results of our analysis of DYS financial data. In analyzing these data, we distinguish costs incurred while preparing the pilot for implementation (setup costs) as well as costs incurred during the pilot's operation (implementation costs). This reflects the overarching objective to describe costs associated with the setup and operations of the pilot and how those differ from costs associated with nonpilot areas, as incurred by DYS.

Setup Costs

According to information provided by LMYSC, the costs incurred during the pilot's preimplementation phase amounted to $337,236. These costs are broken down by individual categories in Table 3.9 below. The vast majority (76 percent) of setup costs were related to the preparation of the facility, including the purchase and installation of new furniture and other modifications to the physical features of the facility. The next largest category of setup costs (13 percent) were consultant fees to MYSI for their assistance with program implementation. Most of the

Table 3.9
Pilot Setup Costs

Category	Amount ($)
Consultants	
MYSI—Program implementation	$45,000
Personnel costs	
Pilot Director	$34,381
Facility costs	
Nonbedroom furniture	$7,415
Beds	$42,674
Security bedroom doors	$52,750
Painting of pilot pod	$38,039
Kitchen remodel	$8,785
Furniture installation	$14,400
Carpet for pilot pod	$89,180
Youth care items	$4,099
Other costs	
Shipping	$513
Total	**$337,236**

remainder of setup costs (10 percent) covered personnel costs (e.g., the pilot director, who was the director of youth center operations).[1]

Running Costs

As the next step, we examined the costs associated with the operation of the pilot. These consist of two components: (1) costs that are specific to the pilot (i.e., costs that are not incurred by any other pods in the facility), and (2) costs associated with the running of the facility of which the pilot is a part, but which are not specific to the pilot. We discuss these two types of costs in turn below to arrive at a composite measure of the pilot's running costs. Thus, this analysis aims to answer two related but distinct questions: (1) How much does it cost to run the pilot? and (2) How much more does it cost to run the pilot compared with nonpilot pods?

Costs Specific to the Pilot

Based on data obtained from LMYSC as well as consultations with LMYSC representatives, the majority of costs associated with the operation of the pilot have been similar to those incurred by other pods. Still, there were three types of costs that were identified as unique to the pilot.

The first category is personnel costs. In most instances, there was no meaningful cost differentiation between the pilot and nonpilot staff. However, the pilot pod had its own director and, since January 2019, a dedicated social worker, which are costs attributable uniquely to the pilot. The costs for these posts totaled $158,680 between July 2018 and June 2019.

The second category is consultant fees. These cover services rendered by MYSI in support of the pilot's operations. According to LMYSC data, these costs totaled $270,000 between July 2018 and June 2019.

Lastly, the third cost category is other pilot-specific expenses. These can be broadly divided into two groups. One is facility costs related to the pilot and its equipment, such as repair and maintenance or IT services. The second group is expenses for supplies and other benefits for clients. In total, between July 2018 and June 2019 these other costs amounted to $7,643.

Table 3.10 presents a summary overview of the three categories of running costs directly attributable to the pilot, including their volume in individual months. We provide an indication of average monthly pilot-specific costs. However, we urge caution in interpreting this value as many pilot-specific expenses (such as maintenance) are of an ad hoc character rather than recurring. For that reason, it may not be analytically meaningful to measure costs over short periods of time.

Costs Affecting Both Pilot and Nonpilot Pods (Facility-Wide Costs)

In addition to costs specifically incurred by the pilot pod, the running costs of the pilot also include a corresponding share of the costs incurred by the entire facility. In this section, we examine these facility-wide costs in greater detail. In doing so, we distinguish staff costs, other labor costs, and other nonlabor costs. To establish the share of facility-wide costs attributable to the pilot pod, we prorate the total costs by the pilot's capacity as a share of total facility capacity. The entire facility holds 140 beds, of which 24 are located in the pilot pod. Thus, the pilot's capacity is 17.1 percent of the total, and we assign this share of facility-wide costs to the pilot.

---

[1]   Please note that the setup of the pilot also likely required staff time from personnel not explicitly dedicated to the pilot, such as participation in training or oversight and management by the facility's leadership. Information on these costs, to the extent they are quantifiable and monetizable, was not provided by DYS.

Table 3.10
Running Costs Directly Attributable to the Pilot

Item	Cost ($)	Average Monthly Cost ($)
Pilot director	$123,456	$10,288
Social worker	$35,224	$5,871[a]
MYSI consultancy	$270,000	$22,500
Other costs	$7,643	$637
IT services	$167	$14
IT rental	$406	$34
Office supplies	$294	$24
Repairs and maintenance	$2,025	$169
Youth/client benefits	$2,754	$230
Client/youth supplies	$1,290	$108
Registration fees	$290	$24
Operating transfers to State Dept.	$417	$35
Total	**$436,323**	**$36,360**

[a] The social worker started working on the pilot in January; the average monthly cost is thus calculated over six months.

The total facility-wide staff costs between July 2018 and June 2019 were $13,816,665, or on average $1,151,389 per month. Of these, costs prorated to the pilot totaled $2,368,571, or $197,381 per month (see Table C.1).

The next category was other facility-wide labor costs, which include annual leave payments and sick leave payments. The total costs from July 2018 to June 2019 were $83,655, or on average $6,971 per month. Of these, the prorated amount attributable to the pilot totaled $14,341, or $1,195 per month (see Table C.2).

Lastly, we examined general nonlabor operating costs accruing to the entire facility. These costs can generally be grouped in the following categories: (1) professional services (e.g., IT services), (2) property services (e.g., building maintenance and repair), (3) other services (e.g., communications services), (4) supplies and materials (e.g., food and food services supplies), (5) other operating expenses (e.g., official functions), and (6) other payments (e.g., grants to NGOs).[2] The total for the period July 2018–June 2019 was $1,074,011, with a monthly average of $89,501. The prorated costs attributed to the pilot were $184,116, or $15,343 per month. Supplies and materials accounted for the majority (58 percent) of nonlabor costs, followed by other payments, primarily grants to a local nonprofit providing some of the teachers to LMYSC (14 percent), and property services (13 percent) (see Table C.3).

Summing up the three categories of facility-wide costs gives a total of $14,974,331, with a monthly average of $1,247,861. The prorated costs attributed to the pilot were $2,567,028, or $213,919 per month. Staff costs accounted for the vast majority (92 percent) of facility-wide costs (see Table C.4).

[2]   The classification of individual expenses is based on expenditure codes listed in a chart of accounts maintained by the Colorado Office of the State Controller (n.d.).

CHAPTER FOUR

Conclusion

This report has documented the first year of implementation of the trauma-informed pilot program at LMYSC. In this section, we summarize the findings, discuss how the pilot program fits with the larger DYS, and provide recommendations for the ongoing operation of the program.

Summary of Findings

Youth Outcomes

During the first year of program implementation, there were few significant differences observed compared with youth on a traditional unit at LMYSC. Analyses demonstrated that youth in the pilot program were less likely to experience a physical response with mechanical restraints or a Level Two physical response. However, they were also substantially more likely to have criminal charges filed, though that seemed to be largely driven by a single month (February), in which nine pilot youth had criminal charges filed. It may be that this was the result of a larger unit-level incident that involved multiple youth or some other series of related incidents; regardless, it is important to note that this is an unusual spike in charges filed compared with other months on both units, and therefore the increased likelihood of criminal charges being filed in the pilot program should be interpreted with caution. There also appeared to be more youth who experienced a side hold on the pilot program during the evaluation period, with no side holds in the comparison group; however, in the last few months of the evaluation, there were no side holds on either unit. We noted that the number of youth injuries spiked on both units during April and May. It is unclear whether this reflects increased unrest and incidents taking place at the facility (e.g., the riot that took place during May), or if it is an anomaly related to reporting of incidents (e.g., injuries were reported differently for evaluation purposes at the end of the evaluation period). There was also no evident increase in the number of staff members who left in those months, which might also have explained the findings. This is perhaps a trend to be interpreted with caution as well.

There were also several positive findings related to both units. Neither unit had incidents of seclusion greater than four hours during the pilot period, and Level One assaults (those that require outside medical attention) against youth and staff were rare in both groups. Also, in general, fights and assaults against staff members were uncommon.

Youth-on-youth fights were common in both groups (experienced by 33 percent of youth in the pilot program and 43 percent of youth in the comparison group), as were Level Three assaults that did not result in injury (approximately 20 percent in each group). Though more serious incidents were less common, these numbers highlight the ongoing need for behavioral management techniques that staff members can use to address these situations. In addition, though use of mechanical restraints was less common in the pilot program, it was still used with 45 percent of youth at least once during the pilot year. That said, staff noted that use of shackles and the WRAP has been completely eliminated at the facility, which is an improvement over the Colorado Child Safety Coalition's report (2017).

Staff Outcomes

There was no significant difference between units regarding any of the staff outcomes examined, including absences, turnovers, and injuries. A positive finding was that no staff had grievances/complaints or criminal charges filed against them. However, we did not have historical data on grievances/complaints or criminal charges filed for these staff members or units, so it is unclear if this represents an improvement during the evaluation period; the rate of grievances/complaints and criminal charges may have already been low. Quite a few staff members experienced an injury (16 percent in the pilot program and 23 percent in the comparison unit). In addition, absences were common. On average, staff in both groups missed approximately three days of work per month, but some staff members missed as many as 23 days per month, on average. And roughly 30 percent of staff left the facility during the study period. This is consistent with staff reports of significant staffing problems and turnover. It is also important to note that it is unclear whether stress, burnout, and vicarious trauma were addressed through the MYSI training and consultation, or whether this is something addressed by the training all LMYSC staff receive. Equipping staff with better tools for behavioral management of youth may be one way to reduce absences and turnover; however, more explicit efforts to target burnout may be needed to have more of an impact on outcomes of that nature.

Implementation Considerations

Though the pilot program was found to have few significant effects on the outcomes examined, it is important to interpret these results in the context of findings regarding implementation. First, it should be noted that the pilot program was not necessarily a fully isolated intervention group. There were many factors that may have led to "contamination" effects—that is, elements of the pilot program appearing on other units at the facility. First, youth from the pilot program mixed with youth from other units during school hours; therefore, elements of their behaviors may have been influenced by these interactions. Second, LMYSC—and DYS more broadly—has been in the process of incorporating trauma-informed principles and the Sanctuary Model over the past several years. Finally, pilot program staff occasionally worked on other units when staffing levels were low, and may have used elements of their training or the pilot program philosophy when interacting with youth on those other units. Therefore, nonpilot units also had exposure to certain aspects of trauma-informed care. This may have contributed to the lack of significant differences between the pilot and comparison units.

In addition, staff members described several challenges to implementing the program as intended. These included absences and turnover, and facility-level issues. These challenges made it difficult for staff to develop relationships with youth under the small group model that was intended for the pilot program. Training was also a key concern, particularly because new staff who started during the implementation year did not receive the same training that original staff members received before the pilot program began. This likely meant that not all staff members had a shared understanding of the pilot program and techniques being taught by the

MYSI consultants. As multiple staff members indicated, these obstacles prevented them from being able to fully implement the program with fidelity, which may also have contributed to the lack of significant effects.

Cost Analysis

Based on the data provided by DYS, this study finds the setup costs of the pilot pod were an estimated $337,236. Once launched, the total cost of running the pilot pod was an estimated $3,003,352 between July 2018 and June 2019, or about $250,279 per month. Of this total running cost, the pilot's share of facility-wide costs accounted for 85 percent ($2,567,028), with the remainder ($436,323) being costs unique to the pilot.

It is worth noting that the vast majority of the running costs stem from prorating facility-wide costs. This is important because it suggests that developing and sustaining the services such as those in the pilot pod were done by expanding on resources already in place in the facility. In this pilot, there were relatively few pilot-specific costs identified in the analysis. Indeed, for every $1 spent on resources only used in the pilot pod (e.g., pilot director, social worker, training and consultancy services, or supplies), approximately $6 was used on resources that could be used throughout the facility. In other words, these pilot-specific costs accounted for approximately 15 percent of overall running costs.

An important caveat to this observation is the fact that, with the exception of the pilot director position and the social worker (for six months), there were no differences between staff resources dedicated to the pilot and nonpilot pods. It is conceivable that different implementation variations could raise the relative costs of pilot provision, particularly since staff costs are a major driver of overall costs. For example, this could include a scenario where there is greater staff intensity (i.e., comparatively higher staff-to-client ratio in pilot areas) or where there is a substantial difference between the staff working in the pilot and nonpilot areas (i.e., where more senior or specialist-skilled individuals are recruited for the pilot).

Considerations Related to Fit with Colorado DYS

From a theoretical and empirical perspective, the pilot program was designed to incorporate elements associated with trauma-informed care models. And in fact, the core elements of the program are consistent with trauma-informed models, including the emphasis on reducing potentially retraumatizing practices, such as the use of physical restraints and seclusion; creating a less institutional environment; training staff to understand the ways that trauma can contribute to problematic behavior; focusing on building positive relationships between youth and staff; promoting family engagement; and emphasizing the importance of addressing behavioral concerns as a community (Branson et al., 2017).

The program model is consistent with the Colorado Model and strategic objectives established under the DYS Strategic Plan in 2017. More specifically, in addition to integrating trauma-responsive principles, it established a more homelike environment on the unit, aimed to use small group processes to address behavioral issues, and engaged facility- and state-level leadership. The pilot program is also consistent with recent DYS policy changes that are intended to create a more trauma-informed environment, including the elimination of strip searches and phasing out the use of seclusion. However, some staff reported that they do not feel like the behavior management strategies available to them through the pilot program are effective. As a result, they described concerns for their safety. Some staff members noted that the MYSI consultants have had some difficulty helping them navigate extreme situations—such as a situation in which a youth assaults a staff member—because the consequences for those actions are different in Missouri than in Colorado (i.e., in Missouri, a youth in this situation would be transported to the county jail). It is difficult to know whether this reflects a true mismatch between the pilot program and staff needs, a knowledge gap on the part of staff that could be addressed with more training, or a difficulty implementing the pilot program and its trauma-informed behavior management techniques given the staffing concerns. However, this bears further investigation, as staff safety concerns likely contribute to the high levels of absence and turnover. This might involve developing a concrete protocol addressing serious problem behaviors in a way that is consistent with the pilot program and Colorado DYS policies.

One challenge highlighted by staff was that facility-wide issues had an adverse impact on the pilot program, in part because certain restrictions had to be put in place across the facility and in part because staff were pulled from the pilot to cover other units. To some extent, placing limits on the programming of the pilot program may be inevitable when there are safety-related concerns at the facility (e.g., reports of a weapon on campus). But it is worth considering whether the pilot program should be shielded from the effects of the problems affecting other units if it helps staff to implement the program with fidelity (i.e., ensuring that pilot program staff are not pulled from the unit unless absolutely necessary and allowing pilot youth to continue engaging in pilot-relevant programs or groups).

Because the implementation challenges may have contributed to the limited impact of the pilot program in its first year, it is difficult to draw conclusions regarding whether the program should be scaled across LMYSC, or even across DYS facilities. That said, there did appear to be some benefits to the pilot program with respect to physical responses, and staff members reported that there were benefits of the program. In addition, research has suggested that models based on similar principles, such as the Missouri Model, have been associated with lower use of mechanical restraints and isolation when compared with jurisdictions that do not implement the model; there is also evidence for lower assaults on youth and staff, and greater education progress (Mendel, 2010). Therefore, it seems that it would be worthwhile to continue to implement the pilot program while working to address the barriers to implementation. This would include addressing the staffing shortage and providing needed training for all staff. On the one hand, given implementation challenges, it makes sense to continue implementing the program on a small scale. However, it might be worth considering whether there are elements of the pilot program that would be relatively low cost to implement on a greater scale. For example, using a train-the-trainer model could be a way to effectively disseminate the training received by pilot program staff to all facility staff.

Limitations

It is important to consider the limitations to this evaluation when interpreting results. First, as described, there were many challenges to implementation of the pilot program; moreover, during the evaluation period, other trauma-informed practices were being implemented at LMYSC and across DYS. These factors may have contributed to the lack of significant differences between the pilot program and comparison unit. Second, even though pilot youth were kept together as much as possible to foster a sense of community within their small groups, there are certain times that pilot youth were in programming with other facility youth (e.g., school, behavioral health groups). This may also have diluted the effect of the pilot program. We did not interview staff of the comparison unit for this evaluation, but doing so would provide additional information about what practices and challenges were unique to the pilot versus experienced facility-wide.

Regarding the evaluation, we relied on administrative data provided by the facility. Several staff members assisted with data collection during the course of the evaluation period, and it is difficult to know whether this introduced additional variability to the data. The evaluation team cleaned the data thoroughly and worked closely with facility staff to fill in gaps and address any questions, but this remains a limitation of secondary data. In addition, our evaluation was limited to those outcomes required by HB 17-1329, given our reliance on secondary data and the facility's capacity for evaluation. Therefore, we were limited in our ability to address any positive outcomes of the program, beyond educational achievement, or to compare the pilot and comparison group on other relevant variables (e.g., risk level). We were also unable to examine changes from before the implementation of the pilot program to after implementation began, or to examine the impact of specific traumatic incidents that may have contributed to increases in problem behaviors during the course of the evaluation. We also did not obtain data regarding specific patterns of service use while at the facility; exploring these types of data would help LMYSC understand what elements of programming may be especially effective (e.g., behavioral health sessions, family therapy sessions). Finally, there may be ways in which our comparison group was different from the pilot group, especially because the pilot unit was originally a unit for youth with mental health concerns. Ideally, future evaluation efforts would aim to identify a stronger comparison group, such as a matched sample, or collect more background data to allow for an approach like propensity scoring.

In addition, we originally planned to hold focus groups with pilot youth to better understand their perspective on the pilot program. Multiple attempts were made to reach parents/guardians to obtain parental consent via mail and telephone. However, only one parent provided consent for their son to participate in these groups, and our recruitment efforts were constrained by the brief evaluation period. Therefore, we were unable to conduct focus groups. However, understanding the youth perspective on the program is critical to knowing whether it will be successful and effective in the long term, and should be a priority moving forward. Finally, we were limited to examining short-term outcomes associated with this program, and we did not have access to data to evaluate all components of the logic model (e.g., youth phase; specific numbers of hours of training by staff members).

With respect to the cost analysis, data provided by DYS include only information on costs directly incurred by DYS and do not include other notable cost categories, including rent/mortgage, utilities, insurance, and workers' compensation. As such, the costs of the pilot and nonpilot pods presented in this report cannot be understood as total costs. However, all these additional costs not included in our analyses are likely facility-wide as we are not aware of any costs unique to the pilot that would not be captured in this report.

Recommendations

Based on the evaluation, we offer the following recommendations to Colorado DYS, which are based on the outcome data, qualitative interviews with staff, and the juvenile justice literature:

1. Develop a clear description of the Colorado Model approach to trauma-informed care and the pilot program model.

The Colorado Model specifically indicates that "trauma-responsive principles and practices will be integrated into all elements of the DYS organization," and HB 17-1329 highlights some of the trauma-informed principles to be incorporated into the pilot program. These include creating a homelike environment, holding youth in the least restrictive environment possible, understanding the role of trauma in youth problem behaviors, and avoiding physical management and restraints. However, it is difficult to know if this is the complete set of trauma-responsive principles envisioned under the Colorado Model, or whether there are additional elements that are considered essential to the pilot program model. Especially given turnover at the facility, having a well-defined program model will be key to implementing the program with fidelity into the future. This type of well-defined program model can be the basis for future fidelity monitoring efforts, as well as monitoring the effectiveness of any ongoing training from the MYSI consultants. Similarly, it would be valuable for the state to provide clear operational definitions of each element of the Colorado Model. For example, the Strategic Plan indicates that "safe and trauma-responsive environments" refer to verbal de-escalation, staff training, sound milieu management practices, safety and self-care plans, and staff and youth wellness (CDHS, 2017b). Providing more detail about the way these elements should be operationalized would provide valuable guidance to those individuals responsible for incorporating trauma-informed principles into programming at facilities across the state.

2. Ensure all pilot program staff members are trained in the program model.

Though some aspects of trauma-informed care are incorporated into the training that all DYS staff receive, the training provided to pilot program staff was tailored to that program. Providing this type of tailored training to all staff—including new program staff—would ensure that staff members are operating from a shared understanding of the program. It may not be feasible for MYSI staff to provide this type of training to all new staff members, especially given current rates of turnover. However, there may be opportunities for train-the-trainer models to be implemented. These types of options should be explored. In addition, it is important not only to provide trainings to staff, but to ensure that the expected knowledge and skills are being transferred. This might involve assessing staff knowledge or skill; or, in the absence of being able to measure staff knowledge and skill, providing occasional refresher trainings to staff members.

In addition, to the extent possible, it could be valuable to provide trainings that are tailored to the role of given staff members. For example, behavioral health staff noted they would have benefited from more in-depth training on certain topics because some of the basic principles of trauma-informed care were already familiar. Moreover, providing staff members with ample opportunity to apply the concepts introduced in training (e.g., through applied examples, demonstrations, roleplays) may increase the likelihood that they build desired skills (Hepner et al., 2018).

Finally, though the MYSI consultants were present throughout the pilot year, there were mixed perceptions as to their effectiveness—especially when they were viewed as more passive observers. Staff members might benefit from more active modeling of certain behavioral management strategies in the moment. It may be that MYSI consultants did not intervene in the moment because they did not want to disrupt the relationship between staff and youth; in this case, the program might consider identifying a staff member who is skilled in managing behavioral concerns to serve as an internal model to new staff.

3. Address challenges in staff recruitment and retention.

Staffing issues appear to be a significant barrier to implementation of the pilot program. Increasing the pool of potential applicants for positions is one way to address staffing challenges. According to staff members, Colorado DYS is already working to improve recruitment efforts by increasing the salaries for YSS positions. They may also consider exploring other ways to increase the applicant pool (e.g., outreach to colleges and universities offering relevant degrees, such as criminal justice). Efforts to improve retention are also warranted. Some staff members interviewed reported that a schedule change in fall 2018 resulted in the departure of several employees; the facility could consider whether offering alternate schedules may be one way to improve recruitment and retention. Providing needed training (as described in the second recommendation) and addressing staff safety concerns (as described in the next recommendation) may also reduce absences and turnover.

4. Explore staff concerns regarding safety and the effectiveness of the program in more depth.

Staff reported that in recent months they had felt unsafe at the facility—and some staff noted that this was a marked change from the previous environment. Staff safety concerns likely contribute to the high rates of absences and turnover at the facility. In addition, staff who are concerned for their own safety may be less likely to implement trauma-informed care principles, instead falling back on behavioral management techniques that involve physical responses as the default. Therefore, ways to address staff concerns regarding safety are critical. Increasing staffing at the facility or reducing staff-to-youth ratios may be one way to address this. LMYSC has already taken one step in this direction by closing the comparison unit at the end of May 2019. But the question of how to recruit and retain high-quality staff remains important.

In addition, some staff reported that trauma-informed behavior management techniques are often ineffective, and sometimes create the perception among youth that they can "get away with" extreme behavior (e.g., violence toward staff or youth). As highlighted, the source of this perception is unclear. It could be due to a belief on the part of staff that there are not trauma-informed ways to hold youth accountable for these behaviors; this is something that could be addressed with training. It could also reflect a mismatch between certain facility or DYS-level policies and the strategies recommended by MYSI consultants, given differences between Missouri and Colorado; if so, this could be addressed by developing protocols that are better suited to Colorado's policies. In this case, the MYSI consultants may be able to provide concrete guidance on how to address this issue, given their experience assisting other jurisdictions in implementing the Missouri Model. Or it may be that the lack of consistent staffing is reducing staff's ability to build a strong sense of community that can be leveraged when addressing concerns. In this case, finding ways to address staffing issues (e.g., through recruitment and retention) may address the issue. By exploring this issue in more detail, it may be possible to identify an appropriate solution (or set of solutions).

5. Consider opportunities to further develop the unique features of the pilot program.

At the present moment, there are a number of barriers to implementation that need to be addressed before the pilot program can be expanded or augmented. However, if issues related to staffing and training were addressed, there may be opportunities to further expand the elements of the pilot program. For example, to keep youth together more and promote the importance of the small group process, LMYSC could consider having behavioral health staff run groups that only include pilot program youth. Staff members also had suggestions of additional groups or activities that would be beneficial to youth, such as more recreational outlets. These suggestions are born from staff's firsthand experience working with youth in the pilot, and they could prove to be valuable additions to the pilot program. They would also be low cost, as they were envisioned to take place during regular programming hours with existing staff members. It may also be worth exploring whether the aftercare portion of the pilot program model can be implemented in a more structured way moving forward. Currently, staffing issues may make it difficult to dedicate a team member to this role full time, which could make it challenging to work with youth and families both before and after release. However, one option might be to begin with aftercare planning in advance of youths' release dates, including helping families to establish needed linkages in their communities for ongoing services. That said, as noted, the initial focus should be on implementing the pilot program with fidelity as it is currently designed before adding new elements.

6. Continue monitoring the implementation and outcomes of the pilot program.

Despite the challenges to implementing the program, there is reason to believe it still holds promise for improving youth and staff outcomes, as it has its foundation in principles of trauma-informed care. According to DYS staff, the pilot program has received funding for a second year of implementation. Given the challenges to implementing the program during the first year, it will be important to continue to monitor the program. Monitoring the implementation will provide insight into any program barriers that persist, as well as program successes and solutions. Given the challenges to implementing the program with fidelity, finding a way to formally measure fidelity is also warranted.

It will also be critical to continue monitoring program outcomes, both in the short term and intermediate term. The facility continues to work to address bigger-picture issues related to staff and safety, and it may take a longer period of implementation before expected outcomes are realized. In addition, the present evaluation focused largely on the reduction of negative outcomes. However, moving forward it will be important to explore whether the pilot program promotes the positive outcomes it is intended to address. For example, this might include assessing youth progress through phase levels and completion of postsecondary education programs. It might also include improved emotion regulation, decreased trauma symptoms, and improved relationships among youth or between youth and staff. This is especially important as the Colorado DYS Strategic Plan specifically identifies the promotion of "prosocial, safe, and nonviolent interactions" as a goal, and the pilot program aims to "promote building trust and healthy relationships between youths and staff and to allow youths to grow and mature responsibly." For some of these outcomes, there are existing tools that could be implemented as part of an ongoing evaluation. For example, the Cognitive Emotion Regulation Questionnaire (Garnefski, Kraaij, and Spinhoven, 2002) has been used to measure emotion regulation in justice-involved youth, and other tools such as the Psychosocial Maturity Inventory (Greenberger et al., 1984) and Weinberger Adjustment Inventory (Weinberger, 1991) have been used to assess psychosocial maturity. Additional relevant process measures or outcomes may be drawn from the literature regarding therapeutic communities, given the emphasis on the community as the agent of change.

There are certain factors that currently limit the facility's capacity for evaluation. For example, many outcomes are tracked at the unit level rather than the individual level. In addition, staffing issues have made it difficult for the facility to designate a single individual who could be responsible for compiling and analyzing outcomes. Therefore, a related recommendation is to increase LMYSC's capacity for evaluation, which could be done by implementing new data collection procedures as needed (e.g., the measures described in this recommendation); developing data tracking systems that could compile all data needed for evaluation, including outcomes described in this report as well as service utilization and relevant prosocial outcomes; and ensuring there are staff members with the expertise needed to support evaluation efforts.

Supplemental Youth and Staff Results

Table A.1 summarizes the total number of incidents occurring on each unit during each month of the evaluation period.

Table A.1
Number of Incidents in Each Outcome Category Across Months

Outcome	July	Aug.	Sept.	Oct.	Nov.	Dec.	Jan.	Feb.	Mar.	Apr.	May
Physical Response											
Without mechanical restraint											
Pilot	0	1	2	3	1	0	0	1	3	1	2
Comparison	2	3	1	0	2	1	2	2	0	2	6
With mechanical restraint											
Pilot	7	6	12	20	9	11	10	12	13	9	13
Comparison	14	14	18	14	18	7	7	11	14	16	12
Side hold											
Pilot	2	0	0	1	0	1	0	0	1	0	0
Comparison	0	0	0	0	0	0	0	0	0	0	0
Transport restraint											
Pilot	0	0	0	0	0	0	0	0	0	0	0
Comparison	0	0	0	0	0	0	0	0	0	0	0
Level One											
Pilot	0	1	4	2	0	0	0	2	2	1	2
Comparison	1	1	4	1	1	1	1	1	2	4	4
Level Two											
Pilot	7	6	10	21	10	11	10	11	14	9	11
Comparison	15	16	15	13	19	7	8	12	13	17	16
Critical											
Pilot	0	0	0	0	0	0	0	0	0	0	0
Comparison	0	0	0	0	0	0	0	0	0	0	0

Table A.1—Continued

Outcome	July	Aug.	Sept.	Oct.	Nov.	Dec.	Jan.	Feb.	Mar.	Apr.	May
Seclusion											
Seclusion < 4 hours											
Pilot	1	2	0	7	4	2	2	1	0	0	0
Comparison	1	0	0	7	1	0	0	0	0	1	0
Seclusion 4+ hours											
Pilot	0	0	0	0	0	0	0	0	0	0	0
Comparison	0	0	0	0	0	0	0	0	0	0	0
Fights/assaults—youth on youth											
Unauthorized/incidental											
Pilot	3	3	14	8	3	5	5	6	10	0	0
Comparison	4	4	6	9	14	4	1	4	4	0	0
Level One											
Pilot	0	0	0	0	0	0	0	0	0	0	0
Comparison	0	0	0	0	0	0	0	0	1	1	1
Level Two											
Pilot	0	1	0	0	1	0	0	3	2	1	1
Comparison	0	0	2	0	1	0	0	0	0	2	0
Level Three											
Pilot	1	0	0	1	3	1	1	2	9	0	3
Comparison	1	0	4	0	2	1	0	0	0	4	3
Fights/assaults—youth on staff											
Unauthorized/incidental											
Pilot	0	0	0	0	0	0	0	0	0	0	0
Comparison	0	0	0	0	0	0	0	0	0	0	0
Level One											
Pilot	0	0	1	1	0	0	0	0	0	0	0
Comparison	0	0	0	0	0	0	0	0	0	0	0

Table A.1—Continued

Outcome	July	Aug.	Sept.	Oct.	Nov.	Dec.	Jan.	Feb.	Mar.	Apr.	May
Level Two											
Pilot	1	0	0	0	0	1	0	0	1	0	0
Comparison	1	0	0	0	0	0	0	0	0	0	0
Level Three											
Pilot	2	1	1	0	0	0	0	0	1	0	0
Comparison	1	1	0	0	1	0	0	0	0	0	0
Injuries											
Youth injuries											
Pilot	0	0	0	0	0	0	0	0	0	13	18
Comparison	0	0	0	0	0	0	0	0	0	23	18
Charges filed											
Criminal charges filed											
Pilot	0	0	0	0	0	1	0	9	1	0	0
Comparison	0	0	0	0	0	0	0	0	1	0	0

Table A.2 reports the mean number of each outcome experienced by youth on the pilot and comparison units.

Table A.2
Mean Number of Outcomes per Youth by Unit

Outcome	Pilot M (SD)	Comparison M (SD)	p-value
Physical Response			
Without mechanical restraint	0.29 (0.65)	0.31 (0.55)	p = 0.88
With mechanical restraint	2.54 (4.47)	2.13 (2.28)	p = 0.52
Side hold	0.10 (0.31)	0.00 (0.00)	p = 0.006**
Transport restraint	0.00 (0.00)	0.00 (0.00)	N/A
Level One	0.29 (0.68)	0.31 (0.58)	p = 0.88
Level Two	2.50 (4.19)	2.22 (2.36)	p = 0.65
Critical	0.00 (0.00)	0.00 (0.00)	N/A
Seclusion			
Seclusion < 4 hours	0.40 (1.03)	0.15 (0.40)	p = 0.07
Seclusion 4+ hours	0.00 (0.00)	0.00 (0.00)	N/A
Assaults/fights—youth on youth			
Unauthorized/incidental	1.19 (2.38)	0.74 (1.09)	p = 0.17
Level One	0.00 (0.00)	0.04 (0.21)	p = 0.14
Level Two	0.19 (0.53)	0.07 (0.26)	p = 0.13
Level Three	0.44 (1.01)	0.22 (0.48)	p = 0.13
Assaults/fights—youth on staff			
Unauthorized/incidental	0.00 (0.00)	0.00 (0.00)	N/A
Level One	0.04 (0.20)	0.00 (0.00)	p = 0.09
Level Two	0.06 (0.24)	0.01 (0.12)	p = 0.17
Level Three	0.10 (0.42)	0.04 (0.21)	p = 0.32
Youth Injuries			
Injuries	0.65 (1.16)	0.60 (1.34)	p = 0.86
Charges Filed			
Criminal charges filed	0.23 (0.42)	0.01 (0.12)	p < 0.001**

*p < 0.05, **p < 0.01

Table A.3 shows the results of logistic regression analyses for youth outcomes controlling for both youth length of stay on the unit during the evaluation period and committing offense type. For purposes of these analyses, youth committing offense was recoded into four categories: violent, sexual, property, and other.

Table A.3
Adjusted Odds Ratios for Youth Outcomes for Pilot Unit ($n = 103$)

Outcome	OR (95% CI)[a]
Physical response	
Without mechanical restraint	0.78 (0.29, 2.12)
With mechanical restraint	0.35 (0.13, 0.94)*
Level One	0.60 (0.21, 1.71)
Level Two	0.40 (0.15, 1.07)†
Seclusion	
Seclusion < 4 hours	1.62 (0.47, 5.52)
Assaults/fights—youth on youth	
Unauthorized/incidental	0.63 (0.25, 1.56)
Level Two	2.87 (0.71, 11.61)
Level Three	1.37 (0.51, 3.68)
Assaults/fights—youth on staff	
Level Two	6.00 (0.53, 68.40)
Level Three	2.31 (0.38, 14.24)
Injuries	
Injuries	1.84 (0.70, 4.81)
Charges Filed	
Criminal charges filed	(not reported due to inflated confidence intervals)

NOTE: Comparison unit is the referent for analyses.
†$p<0.10$, *$p<0.05$, **$p<0.01$
[a] Odds ratios are adjusted for youth length of stay on the unit.

Table A.4 summarizes the number of staff members who left each unit per month during the evaluation period.

Table A.4
Number of Staff Leaving Unit per Month

Unit	July	Aug.	Sept.	Oct.	Nov.	Dec.	Jan.	Feb.	Mar.	Apr.	May
Pilot	0	1	2	3	1	1	2	0	3	1	1
Comparison	0	0	2	2	0	2	2	1	3	1	5

Semistructured Interview Protocol

Staff Semistructured Interview Guide

Section A: Background

1. To start, tell me a bit about your role at Lookout Mountain and in the pilot program.

Section B.1: Preparation for Implementing the Pilot Program (Leadership Only) (10 minutes)

We want to begin by asking a bit about the factors that led to the development and implementation of the pilot program.

2. What kind of local or state policies or regulations influenced the decision to implement the pilot program? How did Lookout Mountain get selected as the pilot site?
3. Can you describe the process of developing the pilot program and planning for implementation?

Section B.2: Nature of the Pilot Program (Nonleadership Staff) (5 minutes)

We want to start with some questions about the nature of the pilot program.

4. From your understanding, why is the pilot program being implemented at Lookout Mountain?
5. How does the pilot program compare to other programming at Lookout Mountain?

Section C: Training and Preparation (All Staff) (5 minutes)

I want to shift to talking about the training and preparation you've received for this program.

6. Prior to becoming part of the pilot program, what kinds of information and materials about the pilot program were available to you? What kinds of resources do you continue to have access to?
7. We've talked to the program consultant and learned about the nature of the training. Did you feel like the training provided for the pilot program was sufficient? Why or why not?
8. Who do you ask if you have questions about the pilot program or its implementation?
9. What other supports or resources are available to help you implement and use the intervention?

Section D: Perceptions of the Pilot Program (All Staff) (10 minutes)

Let's shift to talking about your perceptions of the pilot program.

10. How well do you think the pilot program meets the needs of youth at this facility?
11. How well does the pilot program meet the needs of staff at this facility?
    a. How receptive are staff at this facility to implementing the pilot program?
12. What are the benefits to the pilot program? What are the drawbacks to the pilot program?
13. We understand that the team is a key part of this pilot program. How is your working relationship with your colleagues? [probes] How is your working relationship with leaders? [probes]

Section E: Barriers and Challenges to Implementation (All Staff) (10 minutes)

14. What challenges have you experienced in implementation of the pilot program? (Potential probes: staff perceptions, youth perceptions, leadership support, level of training, need for additional resources.)
15. Do you get feedback about your role in the pilot program?
16. What has helped to facilitate the process of implementing the pilot program?

Section F: Sustaining Pilot Program (All Staff) (5–10 minutes)

17. What other resources would you and others need to sustain the implementation of this pilot program, or to expand to the remainder of the facility?
    a. Are there changes or alterations do you think would help the pilot program work more effectively here? If so, what?
    b. Are there components that should not be changed? If so, what?

Section G: Evaluating the Pilot Program (Leadership) (5 minutes)

We want to learn a bit about how the pilot program is being evaluated by people at Lookout Mountain and Colorado DYS—beyond this formal evaluation.

18. How has staff interest or commitment to the pilot program been assessed—both when identifying staff for the pilot program and as the first year proceeds?
19. Has the pilot program been implemented according to the implementation plan? What challenges have you encountered? What has facilitated the process of implementation?
20. How will you assess progress toward implementation or pilot program goals (beyond what the external evaluation is looking at)?

Additional Cost Analysis Tables

Table C.1 provides an overview of facility-wide staff costs (i.e., not including staff costs specific to the pilot). As described, total facility-wide staff costs between July 2018 and June 2019 were $13,816,665, or on average $1,151,389 per month. Of these, costs prorated to the pilot totaled $2,368,571, or $197,381 per month.

Table C.1
LMYSC Facility-Wide Staff Costs (and FTEs), July 2018–June 2019

Month	Facility-Wide		Prorated Pilot Share	
	FTEs	Costs ($)	FTEs	Costs ($)
July	184.8	$1,147,209	31.7	$196,664
Aug.	176.5	$1,124,801	30.3	$192,823
Sept.	176.5	$1,106,839	30.2	$189,744
Oct.	168.3	$1,068,152	28.9	$183,112
Nov.	169.1	$1,063,873	29.0	$182,378
Dec.	177.7	$1,125,203	30.5	$192,892
Jan.	179.6	$1,128,259	30.8	$193,416
Feb.	177.0	$1,116,5551	30.3	$191,409
Mar.	168.2	$1,085,290	28.8	$186,050
Apr.	174.6	$1,139,765	29.9	$195,388
May	166.3	$1,096,890	28.5	$188,038
June	166.6	$1,613,832	28.6	$276,657
Total		$13,816,665		$2,368,571
Avg. per month	173.8	$1,151,389	29.8	$197,381

Table C.2 provides an overview of other facility-wide labor costs, which as described include annual leave payments and sick leave payments. Negative values represent reversals of earlier payments. The total costs from July 2018 to June 2019 were $83,655, or on average $6,971 per month. Of these, the prorated amount attributable to the pilot totaled $14,341, or $1,195 per month.

Table C.2
LMYSC Facility-Wide Other Labor Costs, July 2018–June 2019

Month	Facility-Wide	Prorated Pilot Share
July	$18,663	$3,199
Aug.	$(10,147)	$(1,740)
Sept.	$2,250	$386
Oct.	$5,232	$897
Nov.	$9,379	$1,608
Dec.	$4,682	$803
Jan.	$485	$83
Feb.	$13,946	$2,391
Mar.	$6,352	$1,089
Apr.	$3,177	$545
May	$19,960	$3,422
June	$9,677	$1,659
Total	**$83,655**	**$14,341**
Avg. per month	**$6,971**	**$1,195**

Table C.3 provides a summary of the nonlabor costs incurred by LMYSC. The total for the period July 2018–June 2019 was $1,074,011, with a monthly average of $89,501. The prorated costs attributed to the pilot were $184,116, or $15,343 per month.

Table C.3
LMYSC Facility-Wide Nonlabor Costs, July 2018–June 2019

Cost Category	Facility-Wide		Prorated Pilot Share
	Costs ($)	% of total	Costs ($)
Professional services	$61,317	5.71%	$10,511
Property services	$135,064	12.58%	$23,154
Other services	$52,228	4.86%	$8,953
Supplies and materials	$623,670	58.07%	$106,915
Other operating expenses	$53,568	4.99%	$9,183
Other payments	$148,165	13.80%	$25,400
Total	**$1,074,011**	**100.00%**	**$184,116**
Avg. per month	**$89,501**		**$15,343**

Table C.4
Summary of Facility-Wide Running Costs and Corresponding Pilot Share, July 2018–June 2019

| Cost Category | Facility-Wide | | Prorated Pilot Share |
	Costs ($)	% of total	Costs ($)
Staff costs	$13,816,665	92.27%	$2,368,571
Other labor costs	$83,665	0.56%	$14,341
Nonstaff costs	$1,074,011	7.17%	$184,116
Total	**$14,974,331**	**100.00%**	**$2,567,028**
Avg. per month	**$1,247,861**		**$213,919**

To arrive at the total facility-wide running costs as well as the corresponding pilot share, we sum up the main results from the previous three categories. The total for the period July 2018–June 2019 was $14,974,331, with a monthly average of $1,247,861. The prorated costs attributed to the pilot were $2,567,028, or $213,919 per month. This calculation is presented in Table C.4, which shows the totals spanning the 12 months of the data collection period (July 2018–June 2019) as well as monthly averages.

Note that it is theoretically possible to calculate "unit costs" of the pilot in terms of costs per pilot bed. This would be $125,140 between July 2018 and June 2019, or about $10,428 per bed per month. However, this is a problematic indicator since costs in the pilot do not grow linearly with the number of beds but rather in a stepwise fashion, typically mirroring the construction of pods. For instance, it cannot be assumed that the costs of adding a twenty-fifth bed (which would be the first one in a new pod) would equal those of adding a bed that would be added to an already existing pod.

References

Abram, Karen M., Linda A. Teplin, Devon R. Charles, Sandra L. Longworth, Gary M. McClelland, and Mina K. Dulcan, "Posttraumatic Stress Disorder and Trauma in Youth in Juvenile Detention," *Archives of General Psychiatry*, Vol. 61, No. 4, 2004, pp. 403–410.

Andrews, Donald A., and James Bonta, "Rehabilitating Criminal Justice Policy and Practice," *Psychology, Public Policy, and Law*, Vol. 16, No. 1, 2010, pp. 39–55.

Ashkar, Peter J., and Dianna T. Kenny, "Views from the Inside: Young Offenders' Subjective Experiences of Incarceration," *International Journal of Offender Therapy and Comparative Criminology*, Vol. 52, No. 5, 2008, pp. 584–597.

Beck, Allen J., Paige M. Harrison, and Paul Guerino, *Sexual Victimization in Juvenile Facilities Reported by Youth, 2008–09*, Washington, D.C.: Bureau of Justice Statistics, 2010.

Bloom, Sandra L., "The Sanctuary Model of Organizational Change for Children's Residential Treatment," *Therapeutic Community: The International Journal for Therapeutic and Supportive Organizations*, Vol. 26, No. 1, 2005, pp. 65–81.

Bonta, James, and Donald A. Andrews, *The Psychology of Criminal Conduct*, 6th ed., New York: Routledge, 2017.

Branson, Christopher E., Carly Baetz, Sarah M. Horwitz, and Kimberly E. Hoagwood, "Trauma-Informed Juvenile Justice Systems: A Systematic Review of Definitions and Core Components," *Psychological Trauma: Theory, Research, Practice, and Policy*, Vol. 9, No. 6, 2017, pp. 635–646.

CDHS—*See* Colorado Department of Human Services.

CFIR Research Team, "CFIR Guide," webpage, 2009. As of August 2, 2019: http://cfirwiki.net/guide/app/index.html#/

Colorado Child Safety Coalition, *Bound and Broken*, Denver, Colo.: ACLU of Colorado, 2017.

Colorado Department of Human Services, *Colorado DYS Policy S 9.8 A: Reporting Critical Incidents*, Denver, Colo.: State of Colorado, Department of Human Services, 2017a.

———, *Division of Youth Services Strategic Plan*, Denver, Colo.: Colorado Department of Human Services, 2017b.

———, "Division of Youth Services," webpage, 2019b. As of April 16, 2019: https://www.colorado.gov/pacific/cdhs/dys

Colorado Department of Public Safety, "Risk Assessment Resources," webpage, 2019. As of September 15, 2019: https://www.colorado.gov/pacific/ccjj/ccjjriskassessment

Colorado Office of Children, Youth & Families, *Lookout Mountain Youth Services Center*, 2019. As of April 16, 2019: https://drive.google.com/file/d/0B9eaXW7_92zSXzc5RVBnQUZyVW8/view

Colorado Office of the State Controller, *Chart of Accounts: Expenditure Object Codes Only*, undated. As of August 28, 2019: https://www.colorado.gov/pacific/sites/default/files/Expenditure%20Object%20Codes%20only.pdf

Damschroder, Laura J., David C. Aron, Rosalind E. Keith, Susan R. Kirsh, Jeffery A. Alexander, and Julie C. Lowery, "Fostering Implementation of Health Services Research Findings into Practice: A Consolidated Framework for Advancing Implementation Science," *Implementation Science*, Vol. 4, Article 50, 2009, pp. 1–15.

DeLisi, Matt, Andy Hochstetler, Gloria Jones-Johnson, Jonathan W. Caudill, and James W. Marquart, "The Road to Murder: The Enduring Criminogenic Effects of Juvenile Confinement Among a Sample of Adult Career Criminals," *Youth Violence and Juvenile Justice*, Vol. 9, No. 3, 2011, pp. 207–221.

Dierkhising, Carly B., Andrea Lane, and Misaki N. Natsuaki, "Victims Behind Bars: A Preliminary Study of Abuse During Juvenile Incarceration and Post-Release Social and Emotional Functioning," *Psychology, Public Policy, and Law*, Vol. 20, No. 2, 2013, pp. 181–190.

Dmitrieva, J., Monahan, K. C., Cauffman, E., and Steinberg, "Arrested Development: The Effects of Incarceration on the Development of Psychosocial Maturity," *Development and Psychopathology*, Vol. 24, No. 3, 2012, 1073–1090.

Elwyn, Laura J., Nina Esaki, and Carolyn A. Smith, "Safety at a Girls Secure Juvenile Justice Facility," *Therapeutic Communities: The International Journal of Therapeutic Communities*, Vol. 36, No. 4, 2015, pp. 209–218.

Ford, Julian D., John Chapman, Daniel F. Connor, and Keith R. Cruise, "Complex Trauma and Aggression in Secure Juvenile Justice Settings," *Criminal Justice and Behavior*, Vol. 39, No. 6, 2012, pp. 694–724.

Garnefski, Nadia, Vivian Kraaij, and Phillip Spinhoven, *Manual for the Cognitive Emotion Regulation Questionnaire*, Leiderdorp, Netherlands: DATEC, 2002.

Gatti, Uberto, Richard E. Tremblay, and Frank Vitaro, "Iatrogenic Effect of Juvenile Justice," *Journal of Child Psychology and Psychiatry, and Allied Disciplines*, Vol. 50, No. 8, 2009, pp. 991–998.

Gilman, Amanda B., Karl G. Hill, and J. David Hawkins, "When Is a Youth's Debt to Society Paid? Examining the Long-Term Consequences of Juvenile Incarceration for Adult Functioning," *Journal of Developmental and Life-Course Criminology*, Vol. 1, No. 1, 2015, pp. 33–47.

Greenberger, Ellen, Ruthellen Josselson, Claramae Knerr, and Bruce Knerr, "The Measurement and Structure of Psychosocial Maturity," *Journal of Youth and Adolescence*, Vol. 4, No. 2, 1984, pp. 127–143.

Hepner, Kimberly A., Stephanie Brooks Holliday, Jessica Sousa, and Terri Tanielian, *Training Clinicians to Deliver Evidence-Based Psychotherapy: Development of the Training in Psychotherapy (TIP) Tool*, Santa Monica, Calif.: RAND Corporation, TL-306-BWF, 2018. As of September 30, 2019: https://www.rand.org/pubs/tools/TL306.html

Hunt, Priscillia, Sarah B. Hunter, and Deborah Levan, "Continuous Quality Improvement in Substance Abuse Treatment Facilities: How Much Does It Cost?" *Journal of Substance Abuse Treatment*, Vol. 77, 2017, pp. 133–140.

Hunt, Priscillia, Allison J. Ober, and Katherine E. Watkins, *The Costs of Implementing Collaborative Care for Opioid and Alcohol Use Disorders in Primary Care*. Santa Monica, Calif.: RAND Corporation, RR-2049-NIDA, 2017. As of September 30, 2019: https://www.rand.org/pubs/research_reports/RR2049.html

IBM Corporation, IBM SPSS Statistics, version 21, 2012.

Ken Blanchard Companies, "Situational Leadership II," webpage, 2019. As of June 19, 2019: https://www.kenblanchard.com/Products-Services/Situational-Leadership-II

Kent, Cara, "Enlightened Witnesses: Providing Trauma-Reducing Interventions to Juvenile Sexual Offenders Within a Maximum Security Prison," *Sexual Addiction and Compulsivity*, Vol. 11, No. 4, 2004, pp. 325–342.

McCord, Joan, Cathy Spatz Widom, and Nancy A. Crowell, eds., *Juvenile Crime, Juvenile Justice*, Washington, D.C.: National Academy Press, 2001.

Mendel, Richard A., *The Missouri Model: Reinventing the Practice of Rehabilitating Youthful Offenders*, Baltimore, Md.: Annie E. Casey Foundation, 2010.

Missouri Youth Services Institute, *Assessment of the Colorado Division of Youth Corrections Lookout Mountain Youth Services Center*, Jefferson City, Mo.: Missouri Youth Services Institute, 2017.

MYSI—*See* Missouri Youth Services Institute.

National Council on Crime and Delinquency, "Juvenile Assessment and Intervention System," webpage, 2019. As of September 15, 2019:
https://www.nccdglobal.org/assessment/juvenile-assessment-and-intervention-system-jais

Peacock, Caroline, and George Daniels, "Applying an Antiracist Framework to a Residential Treatment Center: Sanctuary®, a Model for Change," *Journal of Emotional Abuse*, Vol. 6, Nos. 2–3, 2006, pp. 135–154.

R Core Team, R: A Language and Environment for Statistical Computing, 2017.

Ramirez, Florencio, "Juvenile Delinquency: Current Issues, Best Practices, and Promising Approaches," *GPSolo*, Vol. 25, No. 3, 2008, pp. 10–15.

Ryan, Tony, and Paul Mitchell, "A Collaborative Approach to Meeting the Needs of Adolescent Offenders with Complex Needs in Custodial Settings: An 18-Month Cohort Study," *Journal of Forensic Psychiatry & Psychology*, Vol. 22, 2011, pp. 437–454.

Simkins, Sandra, Marty Beyer, and Lisa Geis, "The Harmful Use of Isolation in Juvenile Facilities: The Need for Post-Disposition Representation," *Washington University Journal of Law and Policy*, Vol. 38, 2012, pp. 241–287.

SocioCultural Research Consultants, Dedoose, version 8.0.42, 2018.

Steinberg, Alan M., Melissa J. Brymer, Kelly B. Decker, and Robert S. Pynoos, "The University of California at Los Angeles Post-Traumatic Stress Disorder Reaction Index," *Current Psychiatry Reports*, Vol. 6, No. 2, 2004, pp. 96–100.

Taylor, Carl, "Growing Up Behind Bars: Confinement, Youth Development, and Crime," in *The Unintended Consequences of Incarceration*, 1996, pp. 41–66. As of October 6, 2019:
https://www.vera.org/downloads/Publications/the-unintended-consequences-of-incarceration-papers-from-a-conference-organized-by-vera/legacy_downloads/uci.pdf

Tuckman, Bruce W., "Developmental Sequence in Small Groups," *Psychological Bulletin*, Vol. 63, No. 6, 1965, pp. 384–399.

Underwood, Lee A., and Aryssa Washington, "Mental Illness and Juvenile Offenders," *International Journal of Environmental Research and Public Health*, Vol. 13, No. 2, 2016, pp. 1–14.

Verbal Judo Institute, Inc., homepage, undated. As of April 16, 2019:
http://verbaljudo.com

Weinberger, Daniel A., *Social-Emotional Adjustment in Older Children and Adults: I. Psychometric Properties of the Weinberger Adjustment Inventory*, unpublished manuscript, Case Western Reserve University, Cleveland, Ohio: Case Western Reserve University, 1991.

Zarkin, Gary A., Larry J. Dunlap, and Ghada Homsi, "The Substance Abuse Services Cost Analysis Program (SASCAP): A New Method for Estimating Drug Treatment Services Costs," *Evaluation and Program Planning*, Vol. 27, No. 1, 2004, pp. 35–43.